WORKBOOK

Our journey from brokenness to blessing...

Becoming women who are found on our knees at the feet of Jesus in passionate pursuit of Him.

Cherie Wagner

This Bible study is dedicated to my faithful Neue Thing prayer team. Ivette, Ginny, Denise, Emily, Rachel, and Anne, thank you for being found on your knees at the feet of Jesus in passionate pursuit of Him.

Contents

Week Four

Week Five

Week Six

From the Author

Even as I sit here now writing this, I'm awed at how God chooses to work through people. Have you ever felt that what was asked of you is far greater than what you can accomplish? Have you ever felt it was beyond your ability? For me, writing this bible study was that task, that journey. At times, I doubted where the Lord was in all of it, and I began to question whether or not this was from Him or just my own desire. More than anything else, though, fear was my daily battle. Fear kept me from opening my computer every day and beginning to type. I felt overwhelmed by this task, and at times I felt like I couldn't possibly produce something worth reading. I made countless excuses as to why I hadn't finished it yet, or why I hadn't worked on it in so long, all of which sounded like perfectly good reasons and other people understood them too. Yet, I could never erase the tugging on my heart to complete this labor of love. Never could I forget what I was supposed to be doing, how I was supposed to be ordering my days to devote time and attention to this work. Each time I picked up my computer to do everything and anything but write, my heart was convicted by the very reason I purchased the computer – to write this bible study.

Know that this book was a battle for me, but more than that it was a joy to write every word. It caused me to dig up deeply covered past pains, failures, and insecurities while allowing me to linger in the healing presence of the Lord in the process. I met my God in a new way throughout this journey. I know His heartbeat just a bit more, and I'm increasingly aware of the sound of His sweet voice calling out my name. Was this worth it? You bet it was. Every tough day when I sat for hours staring at a blank screen, every struggle to compose something meaningful and worth reading...I wouldn't trade a day. I realized through it all that I could continue to refuse to walk in obedience to God and cower in fear from His calling on my life, or I could surrender to it, trust Him, and obey Him in what He'd asked me to do. Had I chose the first option, I realized that the Lord would undoubtedly accomplish His agenda and His purpose, but it would be through someone else. I was not about to miss out on the blessings that my obedience would bring. I wanted to be a part of whatever work the Lord deemed necessary for my life, and I finally understood what I was about to forfeit.

So, this book is as much for you as it is for me. These pages are covered with countless tears of struggle and joy. As I finally began to bow my own will to the will of the Father, this study unfolded, a journey from brokenness to blessing. I began to picture my life as one that desires to be found on her knees before her Savior. And I delight in hoping that you too will choose to be found there, on your knees, at His feet, no matter what the cost.

Hours, days, weeks, months, and even years of prayer have gone into this study that you are holding in your hands, and you must know that much of those times in prayer were spent praying for you. I want you to know that you have been prayed over for quite some time. I've asked the Lord to change lives and bring tremendous healing into every heart that engages in this study. Thank you for picking it up. Thank you for diving in to the pages of this journey that

< 6 >

we're about to go on together. Wherever you're at, whatever place in life you are in right now, whether you're walking closely with the Lord or just beginning in your faith, I pray that you've come expectant to meet with Jesus. He's ready to meet with you. In six weeks from now, my prayer is that you will be well on your way to becoming a woman who is found on her knees at the feet of Jesus in passionate pursuit of Him.

Because of Christ,
Cherie Wagner

What to Expect

You are about to begin a six-week journey through Found On My Knees. Each week will be comprised of five days of homework. Now, before you freak out at that word "homework", I want to assure you that you can do this! Each day of homework will consist of some reading and some writing. I'm a firm believer in the discipline of journaling, especially when it comes to journaling your prayers. You will learn how to journal your prayers to God in this study. You will also dive in deep to several different passages of Scripture as you study. And, of course, there will be some Scripture memorization. Again, I want to encourage you in saying, "You can do this!" When God's Word tells us to meditate on His Word, I believe there's no greater way than to commit His very Word to memory. Get excited about it! God's Word transforms lives. My prayer is that you will experience that power over the next six weeks.

Some of the days of homework will be more devotional in nature. Others will be more prayer focused. You'll read through many prayers that I've written and then have the opportunity to respond to God's Word by journaling your own prayer. More than anything, I want to encourage you to take the time necessary to complete this study. If you can't finish it in six weeks, that's OK. Don't rush through it and miss what God wants to teach you. Perhaps you'll need to spend more time in one week than another. That's OK.

Finally, each week ends with a "Her Story". This is one of my favorite parts. Six different women that I know and love have shared their story with you as it relates to each week's theme. You'll hear from women who have walked the roads of brokenness, surrender, trust, faith, obedience, and blessing, and in sharing their stories with you, my prayer is that first and foremost, God is glorified. Secondly, I pray that you receive comfort and hope as you relate to the different trials they have gone through. God's faithfulness radiates through each one, and that is why they share. Following each "Her Story", you are given the opportunity to write out your own story as it relates to that week's theme. Choose to look back and remember God's fingerprints in your story. He was there!

Are you ready to get started? I can't wait for you to meet Jesus on these pages!

GETTING TO MY KNEES—BROKENNESS

Hosea 6:1-3

About Hosea

I. Seasons of _____ and _____ can often be connected to seasons of _____. (verse I)

- **The Command:** "Come, let us _____ to the LORD."

- **The Promise:** He has torn, but He will _____. He has struck us down, and He will _____ _____ _____!

- **The Prayer:**

2. **Quickness of healing and restoration is _____ to those who return to the LORD. (verse)**

- **The Command:** "Come, let us _____ to the LORD."

- **The Promise:** He will _____ us, _____ us up, and we will live before Him.

- **The Prayer:**

3. **His presence is a _____ for those who press on to know the LORD. (verse)**

   • **The Command:** "_____ to know the LORD."

   • **The Promise:** As sure as we can be that the spring rains will come to water the earth, we can be _____ that He will come to meet with us when we seek Him.

   • **The Prayer:**

Discussion Questions

1. In what ways have you seen the connection between sin and brokenness in your own life?

2. How have you experienced God's healing and restoration at work in your life, past or present?

3. What obstacles (be specific) do you need to overcome in order to fully press on to know the LORD?

Week One

GETTING TO MY KNEES —BROKENNESS

THIS WEEK'S MEMORY VERSE

"Come, let us return to the LORD. He has torn us to pieces but He will heal us; He has injured us but He will bind up our wounds."

—Hosea 6:1

Day One
GETTING TO MY KNEES—BROKENNESS

· · · · · · · · · ·

Day Two
A PRAYER OF BROKENNESS

· · · · · · · · · ·

Day Three
WAITING ON THE LORD IN BROKENNESS

· · · · · · · · · ·

Day Four
THE BEAUTY OF BROKENNESS

· · · · · · · · · ·

Day Five
HER STORY

Day One
GETTING TO MY KNEES—BROKENNESS

"Come, let us return to the LORD; for He has torn us, that He may heal us; He has struck us down, and He will bind us up. After two days He will revive us; on the third day He will raise us up, that we may live before Him. Let us know; let us press on to know the LORD; His going out is sure as the dawn; He will come to us as the showers, as the spring rains that water the earth."

—Hosea 6:1-3

Something that we fear, something that we're willing to go out of our way to avoid, something that despite our many efforts, seems to find us all...Brokenness.

I'm reminded of several times of brokenness in my own life, times when heartache, confusion, and despair seemed to be the order of the day. I remember wondering if God was really there and questioning whether or not I would ever see the other side of my pain, and yet it was in my brokenness that I was brought to my knees in pursuit of my God. This is where we begin today on the pages of God's Word. Join me in this study of being found on our knees, and let us commit our brokenness to the God who heals.

We see in Hosea 6:1 a command to return to the LORD. Although not always the case, I find a connection between my seasons of sin and wandering from God's ways with times of brokenness. Sins bears consequence, and often times those consequences bring suffering, pain, and brokenness into our lives. The sin of pride often leads to times of humbling. The sin of unbelief often leads to times of doubt and despair. Here in this passage, the prophet Hosea is writing a response to God's rebuke over Israel because of their unfaithfulness to Him. Just one verse before, God says He is going to remove Himself from the people of Israel until they acknowledge their sin and seek His face once again. I can't think of a greater consequence than the thought of God's presence being removed from my life! So, Hosea shouts the only natural response that we should have when we find ourselves broken, torn, and wounded because of our sin: "Come, let us return to the LORD." Is there an area of your life that needs a returning to the LORD? Maybe you've wandered from Him in your pursuit of all that the world has to offer. Perhaps it's a specific sin struggle that needs to be confessed and repented of today in order for you to fully embrace Him. Be comforted by the promise that when we return to Him, what He has torn He will heal; what He has struck down, He will bind up.

When I read verse two, I think, "Wow, just two days?!" Wouldn't that be nice to have full healing from our brokenness in just two to three days? Although God is more than able to accomplish that, this verse is not referring to a literal two days. What we can take from this verse is a reference to the quickness of healing and restoration that is available to us when we return to the LORD, committing to Him our brokenness so that He may do with it as He sees fit. You see, God appoints seasons of adversity to His children for His intended purposes. When we're broken, we're more desperate. When we're broken, we're more acutely aware of our need for a Savior. When we're broken, we're more prone to look up. When we're broken, we're found on our knees. It is often in that recognition of our need that we meet our Savior on our knees. What a beautiful picture brokenness can be! I love King David's heartfelt cry of brokenness found in Psalm 51. He laments over his sin and confesses with a broken heart his need for God to restore him. Then we read in Psalm 51:17 this remarkable promise:

"The sacrifices of God are a broken spirit; a broken and contrite heart, O God, you will not despise."

It's incredible to see such a contrast between how we view brokenness and how God does. We view it as weakness. He sees it as beautiful and an acceptable sacrifice of praise. He welcomes it.

We are met with one final exhortation in verse three: to know the LORD. And not just to know Him, but to press on to know Him. Seeking God is not always easy. We know this. The demands of our daily lives repeatedly "prevent" us from pursuing God...because we let them. We often have to push past the distractions and the noise of our cluttered lives to truly meet with Him. That's where the urgency comes from in this verse to press on—to push past every obstacle that would seek to hinder us from knowing our God. Knowing God might seem to be a daunting task to some, overwhelming to many. How can I really know God? I mean, He's God! He's so far above and beyond me. Yes, this is true, and there are certain aspects of God's nature that will remain hidden from our understanding until we see Him face to face. However, God would not ask us to know Him if He was unknowable. He has revealed countless aspects of His character to us in His Word. Read it. Study it. Meditate on it. Memorize it. You will come to know Him in His Word because it is His primary means of revealing Himself to us. As certain as we can be of the spring rains coming to water the earth, we can also know that He will come to us, meet with us, and heal us when we press on to know Him.

Do you find yourself in a time of brokenness right now? Are you working your way through a season of pain? Look up. God is there reaching down to you, extending His healing hand. Reach out and grab it. Commit your brokenness to the LORD, the God who heals, wait on Him, and come to know Him on your knees.

"The best things of life come out of wounding. Wheat is crushed before it becomes bread. Incense must be cast upon the fire before its odors are set free. The ground must be broken with the sharp plough before it is ready to receive the seed. It is the broken heart that pleases God. The sweetest joys in life are the fruits of sorrow. Human nature seems to need suffering to fit it for being a blessing to the world."

—F.W. Robertson, *Out of Wounding*

1. Using the space below, write out Hosea 6:1-3, and then take a moment to thank God for His willingness to heal your brokenness.

2. What area of brokenness in your life can you commit to the LORD today?

Day Two
A PRAYER OF BROKENNESS

Have mercy on me, O God, according to your unfailing love. According to your great compassion, cleanse me from all my sin. (Psalm 51:1-2) When all that is within me feels parched and broken, frail and weak, remind me of your unfailing love and your covenant of peace that you promise to not remove from my life. (Isaiah 54:10) When I am confused and afraid, teach me to lean into you, to depend solely upon you, and to trust completely in you Lord with all of my heart and to resist the temptation to rely upon my own understanding of the situation. (Proverbs 3:5) When my hurt overwhelms me and my sorrow aches within me, gently remind me that your healing work within me is most effective when I'm choosing to trust you. When I'm bound by discouragement and the pieces of my broken heart surrounding me are all that I can see, might I call to mind your faithfulness that you were sent to heal the brokenhearted, to proclaim liberty for the captives, and to open the prison doors to those who are bound! (Isaiah 61:1) Though the weight of my disappointment is real and my pain is near tangible, your presence is more real, and upon you I draw my strength. Because your mercies toward me are new each and every morning, I am not consumed. (Lamentations 3:22-23) Because your love is better than life, my lips will praise you. (Psalm 63:3) Because you, O Lord, are my rock and my fortress, I will wait upon you, and I will not be shaken. (Psalm 62:1-2) Because you have promised to complete the good work you have started in me (Philippians 1:6), I will trust you in my brokenness that you will use even this for my good and that you will glorify yourself through my life. (Romans 8:28) Help me to believe that not one ounce of pain, not one hour of brokenness, not one season of discouragement is wasted when I choose to unite myself with you and your purposes. You alone are able to create wholeness out of my brokenness, to make beauty from my ashes. May I not withhold a single fiber of my being from your healing embrace. Although it is impossible for me to piece back together what has been shattered and torn, there is not one thing that is impossible for you. (Matthew 19:26) So as I continue in this brokenness for however long you see fit, meet me with your spoken Word, and sing over me, "My grace is sufficient for you." (2 Corinthians 12:9)

1. How have you experienced the comfort of God's presence in your own brokenness?

2. Choosing a few of the verses used above, journal your own prayer of brokenness to the Lord.

3. Is there one person in your life that needs the hope that is found in God's Word? Who can you share this prayer with?

Day Three
WAITING ON THE LORD IN BROKENNESS

"In the morning, O LORD, you hear my voice; in the morning I lay my requests before you, and wait in expectation."

—Psalm 5:3

It was a few years ago now, but I remember it like it was just yesterday. I was sitting in a Bible study among several other ladies, and the teacher gave us all a challenge that changed my approach to studying God's Word forever. It was a simple challenge but has had profound impact on my life since. She asked us to open our Bibles and on the inside of the front cover write these words, "I expect you, Jesus." Short and simple, but powerfully profound. The challenge was to come with a heart of expectancy whenever we engaged in the reading of God's Word. Rather than approaching it as an obligation, a duty, a task, or even something ordinary that we're quite familiar with, come expectant to meet with a Holy God, expectant for Him to speak, and expectant to be changed by His presence. Although a simple statement, I had never thought about it that way before. I enthusiastically wrote those words in the front of my own Bible, and every time I see them I'm reminded of the attitude of heart that I should have when I approach the Lord and His Word.

This week, we have been concentrating on the theme of brokenness. We read earlier that although not always the case, often times our seasons of wandering and sin are directly linked to our seasons of brokenness. We were reminded of God's promise to heal and to restore what has been broken, and we were challenged to respond to God's Word by returning to the LORD with all of our hearts. It can be so difficult, though to press on to know the LORD in seasons of brokenness. I think every single one of us would agree that while in the brokenness, we just long for it to be over. We cry out to the Lord to heal quickly and to restore immediately. "Wait" is the answer that we fear most. Yet, over and over again in the Bible we see the command to wait on the Lord. Why must we wait? Why must the waiting last so long?

I did a quick search through Scripture to find every verse that references waiting on the Lord. Amazed at the results I found, I must share them with you. First and foremost, we can see in God's Word that waiting on the Lord is a command, not a suggestion. God tells us to wait on Him. Why? Because waiting on the Lord produces faithfulness in us and stirs the heart of God to lavish us with His blessings. Again and again I read of the promises of God to those who wait on Him. He promises His help and protection to those who wait (Psalm 33:20). He promises to hear the cries of those who wait on Him, and in turn He promises that we will hear His voice when He answers our cries (Psalm 38:15, Psalm 40:1). He promises that hope can be found in His Word while we wait for Him (Psalm 130:5-6). He promises deliverance to those who wait on Him (Proverbs 20:22). He promises blessing to those who wait on the Lord (Isaiah 30:18). And finally, probably one of my personal favorites, He promises renewed strength to those who wait on the Lord (Isaiah 40:31). What stands out to me in all of the above verses is the consistency in His promises. The broken heart, the hurting soul, the desperate one...all are in need of each one of these promises. Isn't in comforting to know that God is acutely aware of our every need, and promises to meet each need while we wait on Him? It is in the waiting that we grow accustomed to the sound of His voice. It is in the waiting that we learn to fully rely on Him to meet our every need. It is in the waiting that often times produces within us a confident expectation for the Lord (Micah 7:7).

Do you find yourself in a season of waiting, wondering if and when God will show up? Find hope today in His Word, and run to Him each morning with great expectancy that He will fulfill His promises to you. Join with me today in saying, "I will wait for you, Jesus, and while I wait, I will expect you."

1. What is your response to the challenge to "expect Jesus" every time to you approach His Word?

2. Read through Psalm 37. Each verse calls us to either trust the Lord or to wait on Him. Underline each verse that addresses in any way "waiting on the Lord" and write at least one of them below.

3. *Journal a prayer of response to the Lord, committing to Him that you will expect Him and that you will choose to wait on Him.*

Day Four
THE BEAUTY OF BROKENNESS

"For you will not delight in sacrifice, or I would give it; you will not be pleased with a burnt offering. The sacrifices of God are a broken spirit; a broken and contrite heart, O God, you will not despise."
—Psalm 51:16-17

Quite possibly the Psalm that I have frequented the most is Psalm 51. Perhaps because I find myself in desperate need of God's forgiveness regularly, or maybe because I have lots to confess and lack the words appropriate to cry out to the Lord. Whatever the reason that draws me repeatedly to this heartfelt plea for God's mercy, I am nonetheless indebted to King David, who under the inspiration of the Holy Spirit penned these beautiful words of brokenness and confession.

You might remember well the story linked to this Psalm. David, King of Israel, fell into adultery with Uriah the Hittite's wife (Bathsheba), and she became pregnant by David. Since her husband was away in battle, there was no possibility that this child could be his. To cover up this sin, David had Uriah sent to the front lines of battle, thus sealing his fate. Uriah was killed, leaving David now guilty of adultery and murder. Although David had done what he felt was needed to cover up his sin, God was not fooled. The prophet Nathan was sent by God with a harsh rebuke for David for his horrific sin, and the beautiful words of Psalm 51 are the result of this divine confrontation. Stop right now, grab your Bible, and read Psalm 51 for yourself.

God is able to make beauty out of brokenness. A heart that is in agreement with God over the matter of sin is one that God takes great delight in. The sacrifice that God desires that we bring is a broken and contrite heart, a heart that is grieved over personal sin. This Godly sorrow produces true repentance, a complete turning from sin. This is beautiful. This is the desire of God's heart, that our hearts would break over everything that breaks His heart.

Praise fills my heart as I type these words, knowing that God is able to make beautiful things out of us, even the ugliest parts of our brokenness.

"For He who began a good work in you will bring it to completion at the day of Christ Jesus."
—Philippians 1:6

1. **Which verse in Psalm 51 resonates with you most? Why?**

2. **Using the words of Psalm 51, journal your own prayer of confession and repentance to the Lord.**

3. **Reflect on God's faithfulness—how have you seen God turn your brokenness into something beautiful?**

Day Five

HER STORY

"Praise be to the God and Father of our Lord Jesus Christ, the Father of compassion and the God of all comfort, who comforts us in all our troubles, so that we can comfort those in any trouble with the comfort we ourselves have received from God."

—2 Corinthians 1:3-4

There seem to be too many things in this life that we simply don't understand. We exhaust ourselves wrestling with God, desperate for an answer to our questions, and sometimes we're left wondering. Sometimes we feel that He simply has gone silent, and that our cries to Him are in vain. Or perhaps they're not. Perhaps it is that we aren't receiving the answer that we want to hear, but not that God's voice has gone silent in our lives. I know this to be true from His Word. Because God is God and we are not, there are things that we might never understand fully on this side of heaven, but we can be certain of at least two things whenever we face trials of many kinds. First and foremost, the God of all comfort will indeed comfort us in all our troubles. Secondly, He intends for us to comfort others in their pain with the same comfort we have received from Him. Our pain is never in vain. He always has a divine purpose. And this is where we begin Her Story today. Her story is one of seemingly unmerited and unexplained pain and darkness, but it is a story of God's comforting love. I am on my knees believing in faith that God is using her story right now to bring you comfort, the same comfort that she has received from Him. Here is her story...

She grew up in a loving, Christian home. Although she knew right from wrong and the path she should take, she would say that her life was one who "talked the talk but didn't walk the walk". Her faith and her life were simply two separate things. High school was characterized mainly by one significant three-year relationship. Although she knew he was not a Christian, she justified her relationship with him by convincing herself that she could convert him. He would go to church with her when she asked, so certainly he was on his way, right? Despite her efforts to convince herself that this relationship was headed in a good direction, she found herself lying to her parents and sneaking around to be with him behind their backs. What started as innocent affection quickly grew to inappropriate behavior when they were alone. She felt constant guilt and shame, but she continued to justify it by promising herself and God that she would not have sex until she was married. Since she believed that this was in fact the man she would spend her life with, it also helped to ease her guilty conscience. Although he agreed that they should wait until they were married, his unhappiness was becoming more and more apparent to her. He began to distance himself from her, and before she even knew what was happening, he began seeing another girl. She would catch him in lies, but he would quickly defend himself and convince her that she was the only one. Not wanting to believe what seemed to be true, she clung to the hope that she was supposed to be with him. He was the only guy she had ever loved. She had to believe that her love could change him. It must! He was so close to understanding faith. His dad already referred to her as a part of their family. This was meant to be, right?

But the guilt remained as she continued to cross boundaries with him, desperately seeking to keep his affection. Then, what seemed unimaginable happened. Making her heartache a public event, he broke up with her in front of all of their friends just days before their Senior Prom. Devastated, humiliated, and completely broken, she left alone. Those who she thought were her friends stood beside him and watched her walk away. As thoughts of shame, regret, and pain raced through her head, she climbed into her car shaking, sobbing, and wondering how God could let this happen. At that moment, as if God were speaking out loud to her, she faintly heard the words to Matt Redman's song "Never Let Go" on the radio. For the first time in years, she felt God's peace wash over her. In her brokenness, God met her there and reminded her of His love. That night was the beginning of the hardest yet most amazing journey building her relationship with God. She had to learn to be content with just Jesus. She wanted to be in a relationship and feel loved again, but she knew it would take time for her heart to heal. She had no idea that her life was about to be changed forever.

High school seemed to be a distant memory now as she was pushing through her first semester of college. Early one morning in December of 2006, her first week of college finals, she woke up with the worst headache she'd ever had. It was as if she had been hit in the back of her head with a baseball bat. The next two days were nothing but a blur. She only remembers being told that her mother was trying to wake her up, but she wouldn't wake. Panicked, her mom screamed and told her sister to call 911. She was rushed to the ER and diagnosed with viral meningitis. Doctors said it was the worst case they had seen all year. She doesn't remember that week in the hospital at all, but her parents told her that she reverted back to the state of a four year old. She didn't recognize her closest friends when they came to visit. Once they sent her home, she was under constant supervision. She couldn't do anything for herself because she was too weak. Her memory had been so damaged by the virus that she would look at something very familiar like an orange and have no idea what it was. Her mom would talk about something that had just happened a few years before, but it was like she was hearing about it for the first time.

Although her memory began to repair itself, the virus had depleted her brain of serotonin. And like she had never known before, the darkness and weight of depression and anxiety set in. Most days seemed better to just stay in bed and cry. She didn't care about anything anymore. Exhaustion and brokenness were her only companions. She felt like she would fall apart at any given moment. Thoughts of death began to torment her. Being around people only seemed to make it worse. Her doctor advised her to start taking antidepressants, but her parents didn't think this was the best idea. She wasn't sure how she felt about it either. There was a battle going on inside of her. She didn't really need happy pills, did she? Her parents told her to just exercise and eat healthier. Why did she feel like giving up?

One of the most vital pieces of her journey through all of this was her relationship with Jake. When he heard of her illness, he came to visit her in the hospital and contacted her family daily to see how she was recovering. The timing of her illness caused her to miss all of her finals, so Jake stayed by her side helping her study for each test. She wasn't allowed to drive because of her illness, so Jake drove her to complete all of her finals. She still remembers when her mom looked at her and said, "That boy was so worried about you. He must really care about you." It didn't take long for Jake to pursue a dating relationship with her. She had such a confidence in this relationship, so different from the one before. As she grew closer to Jake's family, she came to find out that Jake's mom suffered from bipolar disorder and was medicated for it. His mom encouraged her to see a doctor and seek treatment for her depression. She was still so unsure, but his mom said that people with mood disorders need help just as much as people with diabetes need insulin. All she wanted was some kind of relief from the pain that consumed her. They prayed together and made an appointment.

After the trauma her brain had suffered, it took many different medications and extreme faith in God to keep pressing on. The highs and lows and constant pain caused her to contemplate ending it all one night. She just wanted the pain to go away, and she had never felt so alone. No one understood her. How could they? Her friends treated her differently, and her family felt like they had to walk on eggshells around her. She found herself asking, "Why should I even be here?" As she reached for the pills that night seeking an end to her pain, she literally felt God pull her hand back and whisper, "I am here." Feeling His presence and imagining Him beside her in her darkness, she wept as she began to believe again. She knew He wouldn't want her to give up. He had plans for her. She had to trust Him.

She was slowly learning to trust God more and more, but that didn't mean that life got any easier. After dating Jake for almost two years, he ended the relationship because she was pushing marriage as an escape from her pain. She thought it would be the answer to all of her problems, but what she really needed was to make God the priority in her life again. She came to find out later that Jake knew that all along. He never wanted to hurt her or be apart from her, but if letting her go would push her back towards Jesus so that she could heal and feel whole as an individual again, he was willing to sacrifice his happiness for her healing. He knew she just needed time to focus on God and be content with who He created her to be. He cared more about her and her relationship with God than about himself. What an incredible picture of God's love! That is when she knew without a doubt that he was the man God had designed for her. They were married one year later.

Of course, her story doesn't end there. She has had the privilege of sharing her story with many women, and she has seen God use the worst moments in her life for good. God's faithfulness in her past serves as a daily reminder to her now as she is currently dealing with postpartum depression. The hardest of times in her life brought out some of the most beautiful blessings: true friends, a supportive husband, and a beautiful baby girl. Although it's not easy, she chooses to fall back on this foundation: true faith *is knowing that even in her darkest night, God remains by her side, and He has a divine purpose for everything. Her story is one of courage. Her story demonstrates unwavering faith in a faithful God despite the most difficult circumstances.*

I am blessed and honored to call her my friend. Her persistence and endurance humbles me and continually points me towards Christ as she daily seeks to be a woman who is found on her knees at the feet of her Savior in passionate pursuit of Him. God is making something beautiful out of the brokenness. Melissa, you are beautiful, and the Lord takes great delight in you. He rejoices over you with singing. Thank you, dear friend for sharing your story and sharing the comfort that God has given you with women who need to hear it. I love you.

Your Story

How have you seen the theme of brokenness woven throughout your life? How has Jesus met you in its depths and brought healing and freedom? Write out your story of brokenness.

OFFERING GOD THE PIECES—SURRENDER

2 Kings 4:1-7

1. We all face times of _____ _____. (verse 1)

2. God needs only _____ _____ _____. (verse 2)

3. God does only _____ _____ _____. (verses 3-5)

4. God fills only _____ _____ _____. (verses 6-7)

Discussion Questions

1. What was the most meaningful time of devotion for you in your homework last week?

2. What does absolute surrender look like for you?

3. Read Matthew 11:25-30 as a group. Name the command. Name the promise. Name the condition.

4. What is God asking you to surrender to Him tonight? ("God needs only what we have and fills only what we offer") Partner with someone at your table and pray for each other to surrender every broken piece to the Lord.

Week Two

OFFERING GOD THE PIECES —SURRENDER

THIS WEEK'S MEMORY VERSE

"Humble yourselves, therefore, under God's mighty hand, that He may lift you up in due time. Cast all your anxiety on Him because He cares for you."

—I Peter 5:6-7

Day One
OFFERING GOD THE PIECES—SURRENDER

• • • • • • • • •

Day Two
A PRAYER OF SURRENDER

• • • • • • • • •

Day Three
PURSUING THE NEW LIFE IN CHRIST

• • • • • • • • •

Day Four
THE BEAUTY OF SURRENDER

• • • • • • • • •

Day Five
HER STORY

Day One
OFFERING GOD THE PIECES—SURRENDER

Today we are moving from the theme of brokenness to surrender. That is what the Christian life is all about—moving forward, daily stepping closer to Jesus and being made more like Him. As I think about what it means to truly surrender our lives to God, I'm reminded of the precious words of an old hymn, written by Judson W. Van DeVenter—one that speaks so beautifully of surrender:

All to Jesus I surrender, all to Him I freely give.
I will ever love and trust Him, in His presence daily live.

(Chorus)
I surrender all, I surrender all,
All to Thee my blessed Savior, I surrender all.

All to Jesus I surrender, humbly at His feet I bow.
Worldly pleasures all forsaken, take me Jesus, take me now.

(Chorus)

All to Jesus I surrender, make me Savior wholly Thine.
Let me feel the Holy Spirit, truly know that Thou art mine.

(Chorus)

All to Jesus I surrender, Lord I give myself to Thee.
Fill me with Thy love and power, let Thy blessing fall on me.

(Chorus)

All to Jesus I surrender, now I feel the sacred flame.
O the joy of full salvation, glory, glory to His name!

Can't you just hear the beautiful tune? What an amazing scene of surrender: humbly bowing at the feet of Jesus and forsaking all worldly pleasures, everything of our own desires and wants

< 31 >

that exalts itself above Christ. The words of this melody speak surrender far better than I ever could. I find myself singing this song often, desiring that the words would truly be my heart's desire. Living out the words of this song, however, is quite a different story, isn't it?

True surrender is difficult, desperate, and exhausting. It's a battle of our own will against what we know to be right. When we find ourselves in the vulnerable state of brokenness, surrender may seem impossible. It might seem inconceivable that God would require us to offer Him our broken pieces and to trust Him with the outcome. Yet, if we recall God's faithfulness to us in our past, our faith could be so ignited to be able to trust Him with our present and with our future.

Have you ever rehearsed the faithfulness of God in your life? Think about it. Look back over the span of your life, and allow yourself to see how God has provided, how He has pulled you through, how He has repeatedly drawn you back to Himself, how He has answered prayer. Try it. You'll be amazed at how greatly your capacity to trust the Lord will be increased if you would but choose to rehearse His faithfulness in your own life!

Follow me to a beloved portion of Scripture, 1 Peter 5:6-7.

"Humble yourselves, therefore, under the mighty hand of God so that at the proper time He may exalt you, casting all your anxieties on Him, because He cares for you."

It never ceases to amaze me how practical and fitting God's Word is to every situation I find myself in. His Word speaks life and truth, conviction and authority, love and grace to our every need. Taking this passage in context, Peter is addressing the elders and the young men, yet I find these words are quite applicable to any and all of us.

The command to humble ourselves under God's mighty hand seems to imply that if we won't humble ourselves, He will do it for us. It reminds me of prideful King Nebuchadnezzar, who in his pride failed to give glory to God and instead exalted himself. Daniel 4:37 seems to say it all when he writes, "...and those who walk in pride He is able to humble."

Hmmm...doesn't it seem like a far better plan to humble yourself? I'd rather avoid the pain of God humbling me and instead choose for myself the path of obedient surrender, wouldn't you? Yet, we find ourselves wrestling with God, trying to bear the load of our heavy burdens on our own when He is pleading with us to cast our loads onto Him. We were never meant to carry them; He was.

< **32** >

"...casting all your anxieties on Him, because He cares for you." One of the most freeing truths I've heard in regards to surrendering your brokenness to the Lord is that unlike the people in our lives, God can handle the weight of your brokenness. It won't weigh Him down; it won't burden Him. It will only set you free to a life of complete surrender to Him.

Think about it this way. We use our hands to hold onto things, to cling to things. We hold a very firm grip on what we are not willing to let go. Over time, our hands become more and more filled with things, creating much difficulty to sustain such a tight grip. If we won't open up our hands and give those things over to the only one that is trustworthy and faithful, Jesus Christ, our hands will never be free to grasp onto Him. We can't continue to cling to our brokenness and still cling to our Healer at the same time. Choose to let go. Surrender the hurt, the disappointment, the failures of the past, and the brokenness to His healing hands. Just as His Word promises, He will lift you up in due time. Open your tightly clenched fist to Him, and allow Him to replace the sorrow held there with healing and joy as you sing out to Him, "All to Jesus I surrender!"

1. How has God convicted you today through the reading of His Word? Is there an area of your brokenness that needs to be surrendered to Him? What do you need to let go of?

2. What causes you to be anxious? Journal a prayer of commitment to the Lord right now, casting those anxieties onto Him. Remember, He cares more about you than you can fathom.

Day Two
A PRAYER OF SURRENDER

"Come to me, all who labor and are heavy laden, and I will give you rest. Take my yoke upon you, and learn from me, for I am gentle and lowly in heart, and you will find rest for your souls. For my yoke is easy, and my burden is light."

—Matthew 11:28-30

Heavenly Father,

Your Word tells me to come, so I come. The burdens of this life, the stress, chaos and noise of my days have made me weary. I'm tired, I'm broken, and I am in desperate need of the rest you offer. I'm in need of your grace. People have disappointed me, devastation has overwhelmed me, and my heart aches for healing. So, I come. I lay down my pride that has kept me from admitting my need for you. I turn from every distraction that would seek to keep me from embracing you, and I come. I don't feel that I have much to bring, but I come. What I do offer are the broken pieces of my heart — the hurt, shame, regret, bitterness, doubt...I'm laying it all down at your feet now. My "yoke" is heavy, but you tell me that yours is light. So, I come. I long to know your gentleness and to grow closer to your loving heart. So, I come. Surrender is likely the most difficult act of obedience, but it must be possible because you ask me to do it. You ask me to offer to you my broken pieces so that you can make much out of my little. You take great delight in making something beautiful out of my brokenness. True surrender is what you desire. So, I come. I'll exchange my heavy burden for your light one. I'll let go of all that I've clung to, all that I've relied upon, all of my own self-sufficiency, and I'll come to you and find my rest. You say to me, "Child, come rest in me." So, I come. May my offering of surrender be as worship to you.

In Jesus' name,
Amen

I. What is your first response to God's invitation for you to "Come and find your rest in Him"?

2. As I've done, journal your own prayer of surrender to the Lord using Matthew 11:28-30. Pray God's Word.

Day Three
PURSUING THE NEW LIFE IN CHRIST

If there is anything I love, it's studying God's Word. Every day of my life, I want to be found in pursuit of my King. I want the words I write to point hearts towards Christ. Will you join me in this pursuit?

Romans 12:1-3 says:

"Therefore, I urge you, brothers, in view of God's mercy, to offer your bodies as living sacrifices, holy and pleasing to God—this is your spiritual act of worship. Do not conform any longer to the pattern of this world, but be transformed by the renewing of your mind. Then you will be able to test and approve what God's will is—His good, pleasing and perfect will. For by the grace given me I say to every one of you: Do not think of yourself more highly than you ought, but rather think of yourself with sober judgment, in accordance with the measure of faith God has given you."

In this passage, we see that the new life in Christ chooses to sacrifice self (verse 1). Someone who has surrendered their life to the Lord and now has His new life inside of them begins to let go of past desires, wants, attitudes, and lifestyle and instead chooses to worship the Lord through sacrifice. This choice to sacrifice is not only worship that is pleasing to God, but it is a right response to His mercy that you have received (verse 1).

Have you ever felt utterly spent after a time or season of ministry or giving of yourself for another? This is because self was sacrificed. I'm reminded of a trip I took to California some time ago. I went with some close girlfriends to care for one friend in particular who had planned on getting married that weekend but had called off the wedding. There were parts of that weekend that were filled with fun and laughter simply because we were all together. However, much of the weekend was difficult as we watched our friend grieve the loss of a dream and face the pain of a broken heart. We wept with her, we prayed over her, and we did everything we could to just love on her in her time of great need. I did not return home after that weekend feeling refreshed and ready to face the next week. I was exhausted and emotionally drained, but that was the sacrifice that Christ was calling me to make for the sake of another. The new life in Christ will choose to sacrifice self.

Secondly, we see that the new life in Christ chooses transformation and a renewed mind (verse 2). There are certainly costs to following Christ, and the process of transforming from our old self to the new self can be painful at times as we must allow old ways, habits, or relationships to die, yet the benefits far outweigh the costs. Rejecting the world and its ways will cost us, but being able to discern God's will makes it worth every single sacrifice. As we allow God to renew our minds and our thinking, we begin to think like Christ, thus living our lives with wisdom and in freedom. We truly serve an amazing God who can take our old, dirty, sinful selves and make them new, clean, and righteous in Him!

Lastly, the new life in Christ chooses to accept who you're not and to embrace who Christ is (verse 3). This is not about self-loathing or worthlessness, so please don't go there. This is about godly humility, recognizing that any good thing that comes from our lives is because of Christ and Him alone. This is about understanding that on our own, we can do nothing, but with Christ, we are more than conquerors. We can overcome because we have new life in Him. This is our hope of glory! This is our joy and our strength: I'm not, but because Christ is, there is no mountain I can't overcome, no trial I can't get through, no sin that can't be erased and forgiven. I am His and He is mine. What a promise to cling to!

1. What attitudes and former lifestyle characteristics need to be surrendered to God today?

2. In what ways does your mind need to be renewed? Be specific. Do you respond to situations in such a way that would honor and glorify Jesus Christ?

< 37 >

3. **Who does God say He is in His Word? List as many attributes or characteristics of God that you can, and use this list to write out a prayer of praise and thanksgiving for all that God is to you.**

Day Four
THE BEAUTY OF SURRENDER

"And He said to all, 'If anyone would come after me, let him deny himself and take up his cross daily and follow me.'"

—Luke 9:23

We meet on the pages of Scripture again today as we continue on our journey from brokenness to blessing. Today's stop: Surrender. There's a visual that comes to mind when I think of the word "surrender". Although possibly viewed as weakness in battle, the waving of the white flag symbolizes surrender and something beautiful all at the same time. It's an end to the fight. It's the end of striving. As I think about what surrender looks like in my relationship with God, I can't help but see it as beautiful. It's the relinquishing of control to the One who controls all things and orders them perfectly. It's the releasing of a great and heavy burden and receiving a lighter weight in its place. It is to cease wrestling with the Lord and to allow Him to lead and guide instead. Surrender simply put is God in His place and me in mine. There's no greater picture of beauty in our relationship with Christ then when we lay down our pride and in humility surrender all to Him. The beauty of surrender is a choice that you and I can make today to offer God every last piece of our brokenness. Surrender is recognizing that God doesn't need us. Rather, He wants us. His desire is for us to offer all that we are to Him.

If we are to come after the Lord, if we are to passionately pursue Him to become women who are found on our knees, surrender is essential. Surrender is necessary. How do I know this? Because the very words of Jesus Himself in Luke 9:23 command it.

In order to press on to know the Lord, a surrender of self is required. It's the laying down of our will to His. It's the denying of self and its wants in order to embrace Him and His calling. What is more beautiful that a life that is fully and completely surrendered to Jesus Christ, ready and willing to go and do whatever it might be that He asks? There is great beauty displayed in a heart of surrender to the Lord. It is a lasting beauty that graces the face of the one who raises the white flag and chooses to cease striving. Surrender says, "Although I don't always understand your ways, Lord, I know that they are far better than mine."

For it is when we choose to surrender that God is freed to make much of our brokenness, to make beauty from our ashes. God doesn't use what we bring to the table; He uses what we surrender to him. There's not a soul on this earth that can offer God anything that He needs. He is complete and sufficient in Himself. However, He takes great delight in our obedient surrender.

When we open up our tightly clenched fist to Him, offering all that we have to Him and for His purposes, He looks at us in love and says, "Finally, my child, an offering that pleases me."

This past year alone has afforded me multiple opportunities to surrender to the Lord. Like many of you, surrender is difficult for me. It's a hard obedience. What I have learned through this fight, however, has changed me forever. It is much more difficult and exhausting to keep fighting the Lord than it is to surrender to Him. Surrender brings rest. Although the process of loosening my grip on everything that I cling to can be frightening and painful, the final release of it all brings such freedom! More than anything else, I know that I want to follow Jesus Christ with all that I am, and I know that I can't do that fully without surrender. So, today, in this moment, amidst this trial, in the face of this pain, I choose surrender.

1. Journal a prayer to the Lord, committing one area of your life to complete surrender to Him.

2. What is one way that you can deny yourself today and instead surrender to what it is that God is calling you to do? At home? At work? In your marriage or in your family?

< 40 >

3. *Reflect on God's faithfulness. Journal about a time you've experienced God take what you've surrendered to Him and turn it into something beautiful.*

Day Five
HER STORY

"...Let the beloved of the LORD rest secure in Him, for He shields Him all day long, and the one the LORD loves rests between His shoulders."

—Deuteronomy 33:12

If by sharing one's story, others can be encouraged and pointed towards Jesus Christ, then I will continue to share stories. I've witnessed over and over again the power of personal testimony, and the most powerful stories are those that illuminate Jesus above highlighting the life being shared. Today's story is one such story. It is a story in which passion collides with surrender. Her Story is one of endless love and devotion to Jesus Christ in the midst of painful, repeated surrender. Typically, when I share someone's story, I write it from my perspective, as told to me. However, she was able to capture the beautiful script of her story in such a way that I feel compelled to leave it as it is, from her perspective. Written through years of faith and tears, hers is a story of surrender...

I grew up in a solid, Christian home with a very close-knit family. When I was fourteen years old, I was watching a documentary on the slums of Calcutta, and it felt like my heart literally leapt out of my chest and landed on the floor. I knew I had to go there. I remember running home and begging my parents to allow me to go to India, and they gave me permission to spend a summer there when I turned fifteen. Up until this point, I knew of God but didn't have an intimate relationship with Him. It was in a small yellow tent in Vijayawada, India that God broke my heart for His people and drew me into a close commitment with Him.

I returned home full of passion and desire to commit myself completely to ministry. I attended Moody Bible Institute and received a degree in Bible and Theology, which of course provided me with little direction vocationally. I guess God knew I needed wide-open spaces instead of a narrowly channeled direction to accommodate all my wild passions! Right after college, I decided to move to Kenya and spend time living in the slums. I adored my time there building relationships with the people and living simply. Being in Kenya further propelled my heart into a desire to minister abroad, but one country alone would not do. I had a fire in me to travel the world sharing the gospel! It was around that time that I found out about a new mission endeavor called the World Race. It was an 11-month trip around the world. Immediately my heart was racing. It felt like a perfectly designed trip for me! After a period of waiting, God allowed me to apply and go in 2007. I spent over a year traveling, learning, laughing, holding orphans, building churches, praying for the sick, loving the unlovely, and ultimately getting totally wrecked by the Lord.

< 42 >

I specifically remember one night in Mozambique. The missionary we were staying with woke us up early and told us that he knew of an orphanage outside the city that didn't have very much due to a recent typhoon that had ransacked their area. There were probably thirty or so children there who didn't have a thing to call their own. He tossed and turned all night thinking about how these children were sleeping on the cold, dirt ground with no beds or blankets. So he decided we would bring those orphans straw mats and blankets to make it through the cold nights. We were happy to help. We arrived at the village and distributed the goods, promising we would return to stay for a few days. When we did, it was an incredibly humbling and joy-filled experience.

The orphanage was not a building at all. It was a tarp held up by four poles. The children ran out and took our hands to show us where they had put their new mats and blankets. They were so proud. That night, I lay on the cold ground beside them, hoping to sleep even a couple of hours. As I read my Bible, there were two children lying beside me staring at me with their deep brown eyes. As I tossed and turned all night trying to find a moment of comfort and warmth, I heard noises of shuffling to my right. When I woke in the morning, I found the two children nestled next to my side fast asleep. It was the simplicity and beauty of these small moments that stole my heart. Although it may not come with all the bells and whistles most people desire to hear about in world missions, I am forever changed by days like that.

I returned home after over a year of traveling to a life where I had nothing. I had no job, no furniture, no car, and no community. I had given everything up to leave for the World Race. Reintegrating into American life was extremely difficult, but the Lord was only preparing me for greater things. After the World Race, the Lord graciously led me to a job in Ohio as a Resident Director at Malone University. It was a huge step of faith moving somewhere that I didn't know anyone and starting fresh, but I was passionate and excited to mentor and walk alongside college women. I have been at Malone now for five years, and they have been incredibly blessed years. I have the opportunity of overseeing a building of 222 upperclassmen women. I have had the privilege of closely mentoring over 40 women, and I thank God every day for the honor of serving Him in a way that challenges me, allows me to use my gifts, and is outrageously fun! Working as a Resident Director has also given me the chance to use my summers off to continue traveling (the other part of my heart). I've traveled for fun to places like South Africa, Costa Rica and Japan. I also was able to lead trips to Haiti, Thailand, Swaziland, and Israel.

All in all, I have had an incredibly blessed life. I've done the most random jobs from working and living on a sailboat to working for a gynecologist. I have traveled the world several times, visiting more than thirty-three countries in my short thirty years. I have friends and family I love. I currently have a job that I get excited about waking up to do. Most people look at my life and say it is perfect. They say they wish they could have my life. But most people don't know the pain I have experienced in one specific area. They don't know that I envy the one thing they have that I've never been able to experience. It is the one life long mystery that I have never been able to solve.

< **43** >

When I was in college, I remember someone telling me that they were married at the age of thirty, and it was the best thing they ever did. I recall thinking, "Gosh, that will never be me! That's so old!" Being in a relationship was something I desired greatly. Even as a five year old, I confessed my feelings to the boy I liked on the playground, only to be rejected because he said he would rather play football. All through high school, I pined after boys I liked only to watch them date other girls. Throughout my college years, I cared deeply for men who never returned my affections. Honestly, most of the time I didn't even desire marriage even as much as I desired someone to ask me out on a date. All of my high school and college years were dateless. I had incredible male friends and was so grateful for them, but I never was pursued.

Throughout my twenties, I was following the path God set out for me. Yet while my plans were great for marriage and family in those years, I didn't even see one date. I started to feel a great sense of shame at my lack of ability to attract men. My insecurities rose to the surface, and I started to blame my single life on everything that was wrong with me. Perhaps men thought I was too obnoxious, too crazy, too fat, not attractive, too bold, too messy of an eater, too dominant...and the list went on and on. I examined every part of my life but couldn't bring myself to change who I was just to find a man.

I don't remember exactly when it happened, but there was a point in my mid-twenties when I had a revelation. I realized that I couldn't explain my singleness. As much as I wanted to have a reason for why I was still single, I simply couldn't explain it. It was a mystery. God gently started to take my heart and speak His Fathership over me. I am so loved by my Creator. He designed me for a specific purpose. If there was something I couldn't explain, I just had to trust that His plans were different from my own. Though there continued to be nights of heart-wrenching tears, God was lovingly guiding me down a path of singleness for His glory.

Last October, I turned thirty years old. It is an age I never thought I would arrive at as a single person. I've watched my friends all marry and have children. I've watched them begin a life with their spouse. As a thirty year old, I've never even known the joy of holding someone's hand. It's incredibly painful. I'm crying even now as I type this because though I know it has nothing to do with me and everything to do with God and His plan for me, it doesn't take away the sting of rejection and hurt that accompanies unfulfilled desire.

But this year especially, I have come to a place of total surrender. It is something I always said I was doing but never truly knew what it meant. In A.W. Tozer's book "The Pursuit of God," he talks about the time when God asked Abraham to sacrifice his son. God knew Isaac was the most important thing to Abraham. As one reads the story, it seems cruel, but at the last moment, he spared Isaac and allowed Abraham to regain what his heart loved. A.W. Tozer states that God in effect was saying, "It's all right, Abraham. I never intended that you should actually slay the lad. I only wanted to remove him from the temple of your heart that I might reign unchallenged there." That statement struck me at my core. True surrender is not the absence of desire. It is reprioritizing our desire. God is so jealous for our hearts and to be the sole fulfiller of our deepest yearnings. Also, surrender does not always promise peace. I still have moments of unanswered questions, deep loneliness and unrest, but it is surrender that teaches me to trust more fully.

My life was altered a few years back by a verse I've read my whole life but never thought deeply about. Proverbs 3:5-6 says, "Trust in the Lord with all your heart and do not lean on your own understanding. n all your ways acknowledge Him and He will make your paths straight." The part that caught my attention was "do not lean on your own understanding." In all matters, we tend to lean on what we know and what we believe to be true. That is what informs us. This verse beckons us higher to a place where we do not depend on our own understanding. Some things are beyond what we know. I found that in the area of my singleness, I was only trusting God with parts of my heart. I was only giving Him partial trust because I wanted to hold on to some of the control myself. I realized the only way to really live fully was to relinquish full control. If God chooses to give me a mate, that is great. If He doesn't, He is preparing me for something far greater.

I share my entire story not to flaunt the experiences I have had but to boast in my God who has so graciously filled a vacancy that the absence of marriage has left. I may have never met the people I met, had the conversations I have had, seen the places I have seen, or learned the things I have learned if I had gotten what I thought I wanted. This doesn't take away the questions, the pain or the loneliness, but I've come to embrace the belief that one of God's greatest acts of love for me has been keeping me single. I am so grateful for a God I can fully trust and surrender completely to.

Her story is truly one of surrender. Choosing to surrender the deepest longings of our hearts to the Lord, content in knowing that He may choose in His love to withhold the fulfillment of those desires, is what displays absolute surrender and genuine faith. Her story breathes surrender and faith. Over the past twelve years of my friendship with her, God has shown me glimpses of Himself through her life. I've yet to meet another soul on this earth with equaled passion for life and love for people. Her desire to make God known is the defining characteristic of her life, and that is the most radiant, beautiful thing about her. She has been my friend, my sister in Christ, my roommate, my teammate, my bridesmaid, and has truly been one of the most treasured friendships that I have. Knowing her has made me know and love Jesus more. Being around her has caused my heart to break for the nations. Spending time with her has ignited my own passions to serve the Lord. This world has truly been made a better place because of her life, because of her story. I am honored and blessed to know her and call her best friend. Stacy, you radiate God's love in the most tangible way. Watching you embrace the broken, hurting, and discarded people of this world has softened my heart for the Lord in ways you'll never know. Thank you for loving Jesus the way you do. Thank you for letting HIM pursue you with His love. I love you forever.

Your Story

How has your story been marked by the theme of surrender? How has God brought beauty to all that you've surrendered to Him? Write out your story of surrender.

....
....
....
....
....
....
....
....
....
....
....
....
....
....
....
....
....
....
....
....
....
....
....
....
....

IN THE MIDST OF THE STORM—TRUST

Matthew 14:22-32

1. _____ does not always guarantee _____. (verses 22-24)

2. Jesus meets us in our _____ _____ and in our

   _____ _____. (verses 25-27)

3. Trust _____ a fixed gaze on the One who calls us out onto the

   waves. (verses 28-32)

"Take My Hand"—Lindsay McCaul

I heard You say it, I know You did

You called me out into the waves and wind

And for a moment I was brave and strong

But now everything is going wrong

Didn't You know that I'd be scared

Couldn't You see I was unprepared

I'm not asking for reasons You hold or the safety of land

I just need You to take my hand

I could have stayed back where I was before

And never met You in this raging storm

You're telling me that faith is all I need

But fear is all that I can find in me

< **48** >

Cuz I would be ok if You'd take my hand

I wouldn't be afraid if You'd take my hand

All would fade away if You'd take my hand

If You'd take my hand....

Didn't You know that I'd be scared

Couldn't You see I was unprepared

I'm not asking for reasons You hold or the safety of land

I just need You to take...

Won't You please come and take...

I just need You to take my hand

Discussion Questions

1. What was the most meaningful time of devotion in your homework this week?

2. What "storm" has God allowed in your life that has taught you a valuable lesson?

3. In what ways have you been experiencing God's presence this past week? How has "He came to you" in your time of need?

4. Close your table time tonight in solitude. Using the blank pages at the end of the workbook, spend the last 5-10 minutes having a "one-on-one" with the Lord. Journal a prayer of response to Him now. Ask Him to increase your capacity to trust Him.

Week Three

IN THE MIDST OF THE STORM —TRUST

THIS WEEK'S MEMORY VERSE

"You will keep in perfect peace him whose mind is steadfast, because he trusts in you."

—Isaiah 26:3

Day One
IN THE MIDST OF THE STORM—TRUST

· · · · · · · · · · ·

Day Two
"GOD, I TRUST YOU"

· · · · · · · · · · ·

Day Three
IN HIS HAND

· · · · · · · · · · ·

Day Four
JUST LIKE JOB

· · · · · · · · · · ·

Day Five
HER STORY

Day One

IN THE MIDST OF THE STORM—TRUST

"When you pass through the waters, I will be with you; and through the rivers, they shall not overwhelm you; when you walk through the fire you shall not be burned, and the flame shall not consume you."

—Isaiah 43:2

We continue our journey together today, moving from brokenness to surrender and now to trust. I love the visual of the storm in this verse – passing through the waters and the rivers with a promise that God will not allow them to overwhelm us. Not once will He leave us, not ever will He forsake us.

Still, trusting God is a difficult thing, especially when the storms of life are raging around us. Our natural instinct is not to trust an unseen God when we are battling a storm and operating in pure survival mode. At these times, we often find ourselves questioning God, wondering why He is allowing these things to happen. We cannot understand where He is in the midst of it all. I know this thought process; I've been there. It wasn't until I finally offered my brokenness to the Lord in surrender that I then came to learn what it meant to fully trust Him.

I must say that trusting the Lord became easier with each passing day as I began to search out His Word for truth. God's Word declares who He is, and throughout its pages, it is filled with promises of God's love, kindness, forgiveness and goodness towards us. But please don't take my word for it—see for yourself.

Let us go together to a passage that you are probably very familiar with. This passage is often quoted and referenced. I know many people that have portions of it hanging on their walls in their homes. Grab your Bible and turn with me to 1 Corinthians 13. Some of you might already be thinking, "Oooh, I know this one! This is the "love chapter."

When I sit down to spend time reading God's Word, I often ask the Lord to reveal something new to me that I haven't seen before, even if it's a passage I've read numerous times. It's amazing how He always answers that prayer! In the same way, I hope to shed a new light on this portion of scripture today and to encourage you in a fresh way.

As we've all heard many times, trust is earned. We see in this passage today just one of the many reasons why God deserves our trust. Whether you find yourself amidst a storm or you've just come out of one and find yourself on dry land, these truths are for you. You may think that trusting God right now seems impossible and far too difficult. You've chosen to trust others before only to find that they have broken your trust. Each time, you feel your heart harden a little more, and the thought of ever trusting another again seems further and further out of reach.

The major mistake we often make is to assume that God will fail us just like man has. We project human tendencies and characteristics on the God of the universe, the one who spoke everything into existence, and the one who chose to place His love on us. He is so far above us, so set apart from us, and unlike any other, He is perfect in all of His dealings with humanity. I challenge you today to open your heart to receive the one and only love that will never fail you, the only love that will never betray you, the only love that is completely trustworthy.

Get your eyes on a copy of God's Word right now. Stop and read 1 Corinthians 13. You may have read it countless times before, but right now, just pause and read it again. Read it as if you're reading it for the first time. I'll be here when you're done...

Is it not the perfect description of perfect love? I remember reading this chapter for the first time when I was in 3rd grade. At the time, I thought, "Wow, that's some pretty amazing love." Ever since then, I often referred to this passage as a "How To" guide on loving others and nothing more. Don't get me wrong, it is that, but now I realize it is so much more. God is defining perfect love in these beautifully descriptive words. He's describing His love that He has for us. His love toward us is patient and kind. His patience chooses to withhold from us what we rightly deserve, and His kindness offers His grace and mercy instead. His love does not envy or boast; it is not proud or rude. His love is not self-seeking or easily angered. Aren't you grateful that God is slow to anger and abounding in steadfast love?

Psalm 86:15, along with numerous other verses, declares God's patient love toward us. And His love doesn't end there! 1 Corinthians 13 goes on to proclaim that His love keeps no record of wrongs. When He forgives us in His love, He chooses to wipe our slate clean, removing our sin from us as far as the east is from the west (Psalm 103:12). This is our God, the God of abounding, steadfast love to all who call on His name.

Now, having been reminded of His amazing, perfect love for you, can you choose to trust Him? Can you choose to trust this Love, the only perfect love? No matter the brokenness, no matter the storm, His love is trustworthy. His love is faithful to restore all things. His love will never leave you alone. His love will never walk out on you. His love will never wrongfully accuse you or betray you. His love will never spitefully use you. His love WILL satisfy, restore, and heal your aching heart. Amidst your storm, whatever it may be, choose to trust in His unfailing love.

< 52 >

1. How has reading God's Word today increased your capacity to trust in the Lord?

2. Being reminded of His perfect love in 1 Corinthians 13, journal a prayer of thanks to the God whose love far surpasses any other love that we could know on this side of Heaven.

Day Two
"GOD, I TRUST YOU"

"You keep him in perfect peace whose mind is stayed on you, because he trusts in you."
—Isaiah 26:3

Father God,

I'm reminded again today in your Word that you meet me in my storm, just as you met Peter in the storm. You may call me out onto the waves and into the wind, but you meet me there. Help me to keep my eyes fixed on you. When I'm tempted to look away and focus on all that rages around me, remind me of the peace you offer to the one whose mind is stayed on you. Teach me to dwell in the safety of your gaze. Forgive me for the times I've turned away from you in fear and doubt and focused on my circumstances instead of your face. It's in those times that I've failed to make much of you because I've gotten so caught up in making much of my problems.

God, you are bigger and greater than any storm I will face. Help me to be still and know that you are on my side. Since you are the One who rules the wind and the waves and every storm that enters my life by the sound of your voice, help me to submit my worries and fears to your care, trusting that you will order my steps and that you will provide for my every need. I feel like the father who cried out to Jesus, "I believe! Help me overcome my unbelief!" God, I trust you. Help me to resist doubt and fear when they creep in, knowing that dwelling in either causes my faith to be crippled. I cry out to you. This is my desperate plea. I know you hear me. I know you incline your ear to the cries of your children, and I know that in your compassion, you meet my desperate cry with your extended hand. God, I trust you, and I reach out and grab your hand. Pull me to safety at your side. Even though the storm might persist and rage on around me, open my eyes to see what it is that you're trying to teach me through it. You always have a purpose; you always have a plan. So, God, I trust you.

In Jesus' name,
Amen

I. What do you find most difficult to trust God with today?

2. Using Isaiah 26:3, journal your own prayer to the Lord as I did, a prayer of commitment to trust in Him.

3. Pray your prayer over someone in your life that desperately needs to trust the Lord.

Day Three

IN HIS HAND

"For I, the LORD your God, hold your right hand; it is I who say to you, 'Fear not, I am the one who helps you.'"

—Isaiah 41:13

In the midst of the storm, trust...

I remember how much I loved holding my mom's hand when I was a little girl. There was a sense of safety and comfort that came from being near her, and when she held my hand, I knew that she loved me. Whether crossing the street or walking through the grocery store, my hand in hers never failed to calm and quiet me. As I grew, though, it became less and less appropriate for me to walk around hand-in-hand with my mom. I mean, what would my friends think? I would look foolish to them. Plus, I was an independent girl, ready to take on the world. I loved my mom dearly, but I didn't need to hold her hand through life anymore. I could make it on my own.

Somewhere along the way, this mentality bled over into my spiritual life. I was raised to believe in God, to love Him, and to follow Him. Still, there came a time when I began to believe the lie that I didn't need to depend on Him for everything or to lean on Him always or trust in Him every step of the way. I could do much of life on my own, and when I was in desperate need, then maybe I would turn to Him. Holding His hand seemed a strange, foreign concept to me. I didn't really think that this meant I was trusting in Him any less, I just failed to see my need for Him...until desperation became my reality.

Unfortunately, my story is all too common. Perhaps yours is similar. You were walking along, doing just fine with God as a pretty little ornament in your life, and then BAM! A boulder drops onto your life, bringing you to your knees fast. The storm is raging all around you. The waves are ready to overcome you. And in the midst of the storm, God extends His hand to you. In His compassion and love, He pulls you back to Himself.

It is trust that causes us to receive His extended hand. It is trust in Him that takes our eyes off of the storm around us and focuses on Him and Him alone. The Lord your God is extending His hand to you now. Trust Him in your storm. Reach out and grab His healing hand. For in His hand is the best place to be.

1. **Where do you feel most safe? Where do you run to when the storms of life rage?**

2. **Read Isaiah 41:10. How can trusting God and walking hand-in-hand with Him become your present reality?**

3. *Journal a prayer of response to God's Word today. Thank Him for extending His hand to you now in the midst of your storm. Ask Him to increase your trust in Him.*

Day Four
JUST LIKE JOB

"There was a man in the land of Uz whose name was Job, and that man was blameless and upright, one who feared God and turned away from evil."

—Job 1:1

I have spent the past two weeks reading through the book of Job. Perhaps one of the most theologically challenging books in Scripture, the book of Job presents us with the difficult question of "Why does God allow suffering?" and more specifically "Why do the righteous suffer?" I've read through the book of Job before, but I found myself much more engaged this time. Maybe because we're in the middle of Found On My Knees and we've just spent the past three weeks studying themes of brokenness, surrender, and trust...or maybe because I have begun to see increased suffering around me in the lives of those I love. Whatever the reason, reading through Job again has been so timely in my walk with the Lord.

The book begins with the description of Job's righteous character. Even God Himself described Job as blameless and upright, fearing God and shunning evil. So, we wrestle endlessly with this question: Why did God allow Job to suffer so greatly? If you're familiar with the story of Job, you remember that Satan petitioned God to mess with Job, certain that if Job was tested and tried, that he would in fact turn from God and renounce his faith. Upon receiving God's permission, Satan proceeded to wreak havoc on Job's life. By the end, everything but the breath in his lungs had been stripped away from him, and even his closest friends condemned him, assuming he must have done something horribly wrong to deserve such harsh punishment from God.

The thing that astounds me the most about Job is his trust in the Lord. At one point, his own wife tells him to curse God and die, yet through every painful testing that Job faced, ultimately he trusted in the Lord. Sure, he struggled to understand why God would allow him to face such severe hardship when he had lived such a righteous life. He mourned and grieved his losses, and at points he despised his own life, but he continued to cry out to God in desperation, begging God to vindicate him. In the end, his unwavering trust in the character of God stood firm. His conclusion was simply this: God, in His sovereignty, chooses to allow suffering in both the lives of the wicked and the righteous for His good and divine purposes. Although Job never received the answers he was looking for in regards to his own suffering, the answer he did receive was sufficient. God is still good, and He is still trustworthy.

As I wrestled through this book, seeking to understand God's purposes in my own suffering and the trials I've faced, I too came to the conclusion that because God is God and I am not, He reserves the right to withhold any and all explanation from me. If nothing else, He does reveal His character to me, and it is in that alone that I can trust. The Bible makes it very clear that God ordains His children to walk through sorrow and pain on this side of heaven... sometimes as a result of our own sin (Numbers 12:10-12), sometimes to discipline us (Hebrews 12:5-12), sometimes to strengthen us (1 Peter 5:10), and other times to give opportunity to reveal His comfort and grace (2 Corinthians 1:3-7). Perhaps it is that final reason that causes us to struggle the most with suffering. In this age of entitlement, we find that final reason simply not enough, not just cause to allow suffering. We also struggle to understand how a loving God could allow suffering at all. Is it not a beautiful thing, though, to fully experience the Lord's comfort and grace? Is it not life-altering to rest in His presence and know His love that transcends all understanding?

There were two profound truths that I walked away with after reading through Job again. First, Satan requires God's permission for everything that He does. Satan does not have the power to do anything apart from what God allows. Understanding this fact alone deepens my trust in the Lord. Secondly, every storm, every trial, every hardship that has or will penetrate my life has first gone through the hands of my loving God. God does not grab a handful of painful trials, toss them into the air, and allow them to haphazardly fall into our lives. As we grow to understand God's character, we come to see and know that everything God does or allows flows out of His love. He cannot act outside of His character. He cannot be unloving. Believing this to be true releases such freedom into the life of the believer. What if we, just like Job, could trust in the unchanging, perfect, and always good character of God and choose to see our circumstances through the lens of unwavering trust in who He says He is? Perhaps we would find ourselves finally grasping onto the hand of Jesus. This is where I desire to be found, holding onto His hand in complete surrender and total trust.

1. How do you find yourself responding to the story of Job? Do you struggle to see God's goodness in the face of such great suffering? Why?

2. How has the story of Job brought hope to your current situation?

3. Journal a prayer of response, asking God to reveal more of his character to you and to increase your trust in who He says He is. Confess the doubt in your heart and ask Him to replace it with unwavering trust.

Day Five

HER STORY

"Trust in the LORD with all your heart, and do not lean on your own understanding."

—Proverbs 3:5

Personal stories have impacted my life tremendously. Some call them testimonies—stories of courage in the face of great devastation, stories of hope when despair sought to overcome the heart, stories of trust, faith, and love. Many times these stories have propelled me forward in my own walk with the Lord. There is power in personal stories because they're relatable, and it's often in hearing another's story that we're reminded of the truth that we are not alone. Someone somewhere has walked down this road before me, has gone through what I'm facing now, and has come out victorious. In realizing this fact, I can find hope.

Recently, I was challenged by the girls in my small group to meditate on and memorize Ephesians 4:29, "Let no corrupting talk come out of your mouths, but only such as is good for building up, as fits the occasion, that it may give grace to those who hear." At the time, this verse was meant to encourage me to guard my tongue and refuse to allow my emotions to get the best of me such that I would sin with my words. However, I see another way this verse can be applied to our lives in light of sharing our stories with others. When we choose to boast on how the Lord has worked in our lives, it brings Him glory and points others to Him. It gives grace to those who hear. Wouldn't you like to be one that gives grace whenever you open your mouth?

Her Story today is one that displays trusting in the LORD. Every reason was given to her to warrant her turning from God, yet she leaned on Him all the more, trusting that He alone is faithful and His promises are true. My prayer today is that Her Story will be used in such a way in your life to illuminate Jesus Christ and His power to overcome every obstacle, every hardship.

She was raised in a Catholic home. Now, when I say Catholic, I mean mostly by association, not necessarily dedication. Without a strong foundation of faith on either side of her family, once she was confirmed, she was free to make the choice to stay in the church or leave. She chose the latter. Her teenage years were filled with drinking, drugs, and the like. Her home life was difficult, suffering the effects of verbal abuse and alcoholism running its course. She sought solace elsewhere. Shortly after high school graduation, she left without much of a goodbye or even an indication of where she was going. She pursued love, religions of all kinds, drugs, men...anything that could fill the emptiness inside. In her attempts to run from everything including God, God pursued her. She had a few near death experiences, some due to her own poor choices and others that were completely out of her control. Yet, mercy and grace were with her. God's hand was on her even when she was completely unaware of his presence. In the midst of her wild pursuit of all that the world had to offer, she met a man named Jesus.

Hearing her tell the story would bring tears to your eyes, but I'll do my best. She was in the middle of a blizzard with her best friend, and they ended up at a hotel. They walked inside to get out of the storm and met two young men at the bar. They struck up a conversation and it quickly led to talk of this Jesus. These men shared the gospel with her and invited her into a life of faith with Him. Instead, she and her friend left the bar and went back to the car, preferring to brave the storm than to accept their invitation. Running again. They drove away from the hotel, but somehow, just a short time later, ended up right back at the door. Now convinced that someone was trying to get her attention, she went back inside. Through more conversation and prayer with these two men, she began her faith journey with the Lord that night.

Hers is a story of dramatic change. She immediately gave up drugs, drinking, and her life of sin, and she never turned back. The way she describes it is as if God took away her sinful cravings for those things that night when He gave her a new heart. She was never going to be the same.

Although she radically walked away from her life of sin, hardship and trials did not leave her. She went on to marry a few years later and have three children. Just about all twelve years of her marriage were difficult. Feeling trapped in an abusive relationship that turned adulterous, she leaned in closer to Jesus, choosing to devote herself to the Lord in the middle of intense trial. She trusted in the Lord. When every earthly thing around her failed her and life as she knew it crumbled around her, she trusted the Lord. The marriage ended, and she went on to raise her three children on her own, trying to fill the roles of both mom and dad. There were many times when she had no idea how the bills were going to get paid or where the rent money was going to come from, but she never stopped trusting in the Lord.

Despite her own needs, she loved others fiercely and gave of herself constantly. God faithfully was her provision and her portion. There was never a time that she and her children went without what they needed. She raised her children to know and love the Lord, to be forgiving and full of grace towards others, and to live a life that is worthy of the calling. She constantly lived in such a way that her faith in Jesus Christ was always evident. It was not uncommon for her children to find her in the Word and on her knees. She was devoted to the Lord, no matter what life brought her way.

She continues to live daily for the glory of God and the betterment of His people. She gives freely of herself to others without reservation. She is a faithful prayer warrior, always on her knees for others. She's eager to share her hope in Christ with everyone she encounters. My life would not be the same without her. She showed me what it looks like to love God with all your heart. She exemplified forgiveness. She modeled grace. Her story is one that I pray impacts future generations; it has definitely impacted me. Her story is the story of my mom.

Mom, I love you. I cherish you. There has been no greater example for me of a life of trusting in the Lord than yours. Your life has been filled with trials, hardships, and pain, but it's a life that has not been lived in vain. You are so loved. You have been a loving mother to far more than your three biological children. I am blessed beyond measure to be your daughter. You have taught me to live is Christ and to die is gain. You've never clung to the temporary pleasures of this life. Rather, you've modeled what it looks like to cling to the Savior's hand. The following verses embody the thoughts that I cannot seem to capture in my own words, so I'll just resort to the greatest text there is: God's Word.

"I thank my God in all my remembrance of you, always in every prayer of mine for you all making my prayer with joy, because of your partnership in the gospel from the first day until now. And I am sure of this, that He who began a good work in you will bring it to completion at the day of Jesus Christ."
—Philippians 1:3-6

Your Story

Throughout the pages of your story, how has trusting in the Lord been a theme? In what ways has your trust in Him increased over time? Write out your story of trusting in the Lord.

TRUST

A WAY IN THE DEPTHS OF THE SEA—FAITH

Exodus 14

1. Sincere _____ in God's character leads to saving _____.
   (verses 1-9)

2. Faith is _____ the Word of God and _____ upon it, no
   matter how I _____ because God promises a good
   _____.

3. Rehearsing God's faithfulness _____ faith in us. (verses 10-31)

Week Four *Teaching Outline*

Discussion Questions

1. What was the most significant time of devotion in your homework this week?

2. Is there a disconnect between faith and works in your own life? Is your faith accompanied by works that would prove it to be genuine?

3. In what ways this past week have you allowed feelings to lead you rather than faith?

4. Rehearse God's faithfulness: What is one specific area of growth in your life that you've seen developing over the past few weeks? Praise God for it!

Week Four

A WAY IN THE DEPTHS OF THE SEA —FAITH

THIS WEEK'S MEMORY VERSE

"And without faith it is impossible to please God, because anyone who comes to Him must believe that He exists and that He rewards those who earnestly seek Him."

—Hebrews 11:6

Day One
A WAY IN THE DEPTHS OF THE SEA—FAITH

· · · · · · · · · ·

Day Two
A PRAYER OF FAITH

· · · · · · · · · ·

Day Three
THE FAITH OF THE BLEEDING WOMAN

· · · · · · · · · ·

Day Four
FEAR VERSUS FAITH

· · · · · · · · · ·

Day Five
HER STORY

Day One

A WAY IN THE DEPTHS OF THE SEA—FAITH

Today begins Faith Week. We've studied the riches of God's Word as we've journeyed through Brokenness, Surrender, and Trust. Now, we move to faith. And what better way to begin than with a great definition to work with. So, here we go. Let's jump right in!

Faith is...

...believing God's Word.

This is the attitude that declares, "God's Word says it. I believe it. That settles it." It is the heart that refuses to replace God's truth with man's reasoning and human understanding. Saving faith stands upon the truth of God's Word as its ultimate authority in all things. Genuine faith elevates God's Word above all else, recognizing that even man's greatest wisdom is foolishness to God. Faith is believing God's Word.

...acting on God's Word.

This is the attitude that refuses to merely hear God's Word, but rather is compelled to do what it says. Faith in action is faith that is alive. Acting on God's Word requires a conviction that what God's Word says is true. Obedience is doing what God's Word says. Hearing the Word of God and doing it are two very different things. Faith is acting on God's Word.

...refusing to allow feelings to lead.

This is the attitude that recognizes the danger in following emotions and feelings. The heart is the seat of our emotions. Jeremiah 17:9 tells us that the heart is deceitful above all things and beyond cure. To live our lives by the mantra "follow your heart" is simply foolishness. Rather, follow God's Word. Believe it. Act on it. No matter how you feel, choose to believe that feelings must follow and faith must lead. Faith is refusing to allow feelings to lead.

...believing that God promises a good result.

This is the attitude that understands that faith pleases God. God's pleasure alone is a good end result and should therefore be the desire of our hearts. Yet, God goes beyond that and also chooses to bless us for our faith. Hebrews 11:6 tells us that God rewards those who earnestly seek Him. Faith is believing that God promises a good result.

1. *What is the hardest thing about faith for you? Is it believing God's Word? Acting on it? Refusing to allow your feelings to lead you? Or believing that God promises a good result? Why?*

2. *How does exposure to God's Word affect your faith?*

3. Look up Hebrews 11:6 and write the words of this verse below. Commit this verse to memory this week.

Day Two
A PRAYER OF FAITH

"Was it not you who dried up the sea, the waters of the great deep, who made the depths of the sea a way for the redeemed to pass over?"

—Isaiah 51:10

Heavenly Father,

You have called me to faith, the kind of faith that believes your Word is true, a faith that drives me to action. So, hear my prayer of faith, and incline your ear to me now. I have trusted in who you say you are, and it has stirred my heart to action. Give me faith to step out and do what your Word tells me to do.

You alone are great and worthy to be praised. You are high and exalted, and to you all glory and honor is due. You spoke and all that we see came to be. Your hands fashioned and formed me. The shining stars display your magnificence. Even the wind blows at your command. You blew and parted the great Red Sea, allowing your people to cross over on dry land to safety. I can hardly imagine the fear that must have welled up in their hearts as the walls of the sea lined either side of them, tempting them to turn back. Yet, it was their faith in you that led them on.

Father help me to see that fear is the enemy of faith. When I give in to fear, it cripples and paralyzes my faith, causing me to be ineffective in serving you and in reaching others for you. Increase my faith and weaken my will. When my emotions tempt me to fear whatever it may be that you're calling me to, help me to choose faith instead. Bring to remembrance your faithfulness, not only to your chosen people Israel, but also in my own life. As I reflect on all that you've done in and through me, cause my faith to flourish. Just as you made a way in the depths of the sea for them, you are making a way for me to pass over. Help me to refuse fear, to embrace faith, and to stand firm on your truth. It is only through you that I can overcome. Grant me the faith necessary to follow after you wherever you might lead me, whether it be to the mountain's heights or the valley's depths. Faith is choosing to believe that you are good despite my circumstances. Today, Jesus, I choose faith!

In Jesus' name,
Amen

1. **Rehearse God's faithfulness. What "Red Seas" has God parted for you, making a way for you in the depths of the sea when you saw no way to make it on your own?**

2. **Using Hebrews 11:1 and 6, journal your own prayer of faith to the Lord.**

Day Three
THE FAITH OF THE BLEEDING WOMAN

"And He said to her, 'Daughter, your faith has made you well; go in peace, and be healed of your disease.'"

—Mark 5:34

As we continue on our journey of faith, today we will take a look at one woman's incredible faith that led her to the feet of Jesus. Perhaps you are already familiar with this story. Whether you are or aren't, my prayer today is that God's Word speaks something new to your heart, something fresh. Join me in Mark 5:21-34. Stop right here, grab your Bible, and take a moment to read the story.

By this point in Jesus' earthly ministry, He was already sought after by the crowds. He had performed enough miracles that people flocked to Him for healing. They may or may not have believed that Jesus was the Son of God, but one thing we can assume is that they did desire the blessings from His hand. Jairus, a prominent ruler in the synagogue, came to Jesus that day with a desperate need – his daughter was ill and facing death. His plea was urgent and required the immediate attention of Jesus. So, we can see that the story doesn't even begin with the bleeding woman. Jesus was already on a mission to heal this young girl, the daughter of an important man, yet the beauty of the story unfolds in the patience and kindness Jesus displays to "just another woman in the crowd."

The text tells us that this woman had suffered from her bleeding for twelve years. Due to the severity of her condition, she had spent all that she had to seek a cure, but her efforts had been in vain. She only grew worse. Not only had her illness cost her all that she had financially, but it had also deemed her an outcast from society. Women were considered to be unclean during their monthly cycle, thus prohibiting them from worshiping in the temple. Not only were they prohibited to participate in corporate worship, but anyone that they came into contact with would be deemed unclean as well. You can imagine the heavy weight of shame that she carried with her everywhere. She was regarded as unworthy. She had little hope left to cling to, if any. But then, there was Jesus. She had heard of this man who healed the sick, raised the dead, and performed the impossible. Perhaps, just maybe, He could do that for her. So she, among many, joined the crowd that day that pressed in to get close to Jesus. Imagine the courage it took for her to even be in a crowd. Certain that others would recognize her and know her to be the woman who was unclean. Certain that her nearness to others would cause them to be unclean as well. But, she had one hope left to cling to, and that hope was in this man named Jesus. Her faith, whether superstitious or genuine, drew her near to Jesus that day. She knew that if she could but reach out and touch the edge of His robe, she would be healed. So, she pressed in further, desperate for the healing that could only come from Him.

As the crowds pressed in around Jesus, I can only imagine the frustration of Jairus. Knowing that his daughter didn't have much time left, I assume his impatience was at an all-time high when Jesus stopped to ask who had touched his garments. Naturally, many people had brushed up against Him in the crowd as He sought to make His way through it. Why would He ask such a seemingly ridiculous question? *Perhaps to test the faith of the one who pursued Him.* Would she stand up and confess that it was her who touched Him? Would she choose to be acknowledged in the crowd for having faith to pursue Him in such a way? The text tells us that although she was trembling in fear, she came forward, confessing the entire truth to Him. Can you even imagine the scene? The crowd at this point centered in on this one woman, a woman who probably dreaded attention more than anything due to the known shame she had carried for so long. Yet, her faith propelled her forward. Her faith drew her near to Him. And it was her faith that made her well.

As I read this story again, there are several truths that I can find within it. **First** of all, Jesus is powerful, and He is able to heal and to overcome death. We see His power on display so magnificently here in the life of this one woman. **Second**, it is our faith that connects us to that power. This woman's faith in what she knew Jesus could do for her drew her to Him and brought full healing into her life. **Third**, our faith can be weak and imperfect, but the object of our faith must be Jesus. Perhaps this woman only sought out Jesus for what He could offer her...at first. Maybe her faith was superstitious. Maybe she thought, "Well, I've tried everything else, so why not Jesus too?" Nonetheless, the object of her faith at that moment was Jesus. She knew she had to get to Jesus. She was focused on Jesus. **Fourth**, Jesus moves at Jesus' speed, the speed that His sovereignty deems necessary. Perhaps this sudden interruption caused Jairus to doubt Jesus and His ability to heal his daughter. Perhaps the woman had struggled to hold onto any faith at all after suffering and waiting for twelve years. But Jesus is never late. Never. His timing is always perfect. He's never late. He's rarely early either, but He's always on time. Remember that the next time you question Him. He is sovereign, and He knows exactly what He's doing. **Fifth** and finally, you will always give and get more than you bargain for when you come to Jesus. After this woman had given all that she had left in this world (materially), she gave all the dignity she might have had left to press in to touch Jesus. He could have shunned her and rejected her for doing such a thing. But He didn't. Verse 34 tells us that her faith made her well. What's interesting about that phrase "made her well" is that it refers to more than just a physical wellness or healing. Jesus not only healed her physically but also spiritually. He made her spiritually well. Her faith, small as it may have been, made her well, and her faith in Him flourished that day.

1. **In what ways can you relate to the bleeding woman?**

2. **What clouds vibrant faith in your life?**

3. **What are you waiting on the Lord for right now? By faith, can you choose to say today that God's timing is perfect in all things?**

4. *Journal a prayer of response to the Lord today, confessing your fears and asking Him to increase your faith in Him.*

Day Four
FEAR VERSUS FAITH

"For God gave us a spirit not of fear but of power and love and self-control." —2 Timothy 1:7

"Fear not, for I have redeemed you; I have called you by name, you are mine." —Isaiah 43:1b

"There is no fear in love, but perfect love casts out fear. For fear has to do with punishment, and whoever fears has not been perfected in love." —1 John 4:18

"The LORD is my light and my salvation; whom shall I fear? The LORD is the stronghold of my life; of whom shall I be afraid?" —Psalm 27:1

"...fear not, for I am with you; be not dismayed, for I am your God; I will strengthen you, I will help you, I will uphold you with my righteous right hand." —Isaiah 41:10

Fear defined: a distressing emotion aroused by impending danger, evil, pain, etc., whether the threat is real or imagined.

The Bible seems to have a lot to say about fear, and other than having a fear of the Lord, God's Word doesn't seem to shed a good light on fear. That's probably because fear is not of God. Fear cripples us and keeps us from fulfilling the purposes that God has given us. Fear breeds doubt, worry, and anxiety, all of which hinder us in our pursuit of Christ. Fear prevents us from absolute devotion to Christ. Fear clouds our vision and causes our focus to be on self. Fear is the enemy's specialty. When we're bound by fear, we cannot reflect a life that is identified with Jesus Christ. Oswald Chambers says it well in his incredible book of daily devotions, My Utmost for His Highest: "All our fears are wicked, and we fear because we will not nourish ourselves in our faith." Fear is welcomed into our lives when we actively or passively allow Christ to take a back seat and no longer be our first priority. When we starve our souls from the richest of food that can be found in God's Word alone, we become a magnet for such schemes of the enemy: fear, doubt, anxiety, unbelief. There should be no room for fear in the life of a forgiven, redeemed, restored, loved, and valued child of God.

Fear has shackled far too many believers for too long, thus hindering God's work in and through us. This must end! Will you join me in standing upon the truths of God's Word, refusing the lies that seek to deceive us, and embracing freedom from the stronghold of fear? God calls us to lives of faith, choosing to believe in Him despite our circumstances.

When fear creeps in, faith says, "Because God is for me, who can be against me?" Faith says, "I will not be afraid because my God is with me, and He has promised to never leave me or forsake me." Faith says, "On Christ the solid rock I stand; all other ground is sinking sand." What are you standing on today? Fear or faith? Fear cripples you; faith frees you. Walk in faith.

1. What fears are currently present in your life, crippling your faith in Christ?

2. One of the best ways I've found to overcome fear is the discipline of rehearsing God's faithfulness. Make a list of the ways you've seen God be faithful to you, your family, your friends, etc. within the past year. Rehearsing God's faithfulness breeds faith within us.

Day Five

HER STORY

"For I know the plans I have for you," declares the LORD, "plans to prosper you and not to harm you, plans to give you hope and a future."

—Jeremiah 29:11

Her Story this week is one of faith that has been refined by the fire. Her Story is one of continuous trial and yet expectant hope in the One who is to come. Her Story has the name of Jesus written all over it. This is her story...

At nine months old, she was adopted into a loving, Christian home. Her adoptive parents were unable to have any children of their own, so she was raised as an only child, knowing not only the genuine love of her parents, but also the love of Jesus. From an early age, church, Sunday school, youth activities, and the like filled her days. Her parents were very involved in their church teaching Sunday school, leading the youth, and consistently modeling their faith for her to see. Her parents' friends were all Christians, resulting in a tremendous amount of godly influence in her life. Although she didn't notice it as much as a child, when she was older, she was able to see how significant her upbringing was.

Perhaps the beginning of the separation between her and her faith was when she went away to college and stopped going to church. Being away from home, her church, and all the godly influences that she had there, she no longer made it a priority to be in church regularly, but even so, she can see how this was the time in her life when God really began His work in her.

When she got married and had kids, she began to see the importance of raising her children in the church. So, she went back and had them both baptized and eventually confirmed in the Lutheran church. It was shortly after her second child was born that they moved from New Jersey to Arizona. Up until that point, her parents were her sole source of strength. She relied entirely on them. She was so worried about making new friends in a new place, but it was during this time that God really began to pursue her. Her mother suggested that she join a church in Arizona and sign up for a women's Bible study. Although she saw the importance of raising her children in the church, faith to her was not much more than religion at this point, just a "busyness" in the name of the Lord.

She found herself living the life her parents had, as far as being active in the church. She was involved in everything, consumed in doing, doing, doing. Her son remained involved in the church until he was about 16 years old, but her daughter stayed beyond that. The faith of her daughter was something she always admired. Even from a young age, her daughter was never afraid to share her faith with others and witness to those who didn't yet know Jesus. In some ways, her daughter's faith supported her own. God was at work in her life, pulling her towards Himself. She decided to attend a weekend Bible retreat with other adults from the church, a weekend away dedicated to knowing Jesus Christ. This is where her faith changed forever. She had always believed in God, but never really took Him at His Word, never really let Him have complete control of her life. She had spent her life making lots of deals with God—"God, if you do this, if you come through for me in this way, then I promise..." But, it was this weekend that she met Jesus as a person, in a tangible way, and she committed her life to Him. It was this weekend that she realized that God was right there beside her, and He always had been. From that moment on, she chose to walk with Him no matter what life would bring (little did she know). She learned that it wasn't about making deals with God, it was about receiving His grace. There was nothing she could do to earn it; she just needed to receive it.

For the majority of her life, she struggled with severe health issues. Many of these issues went untreated for years, as doctors were simply unable to correctly diagnose her. Not only has she constantly faced sickness in her own life but also in the lives of her parents. When she was just 8 years old, her mother developed breast cancer. She can remember praying to God on her knees, begging Him to not let her mother die. There seemed to be so much emphasis on death, which instilled great fear in her heart. What if she did something wrong, would God then take her mother? Her mother survived the breast cancer, but her breasts did not. She had a double mastectomy and ended up developing skin cancer at the site of her breast cancer. Her mother beat that cancer as well, but eventually developed lung cancer. All she could think was how unfair this was. Her mother had never smoked a day in her life. How could these horrible cancers continue to find her mother? She visited her mom every single day in the hospital, often times spending the night there. Her mom didn't want anyone to know that she was dying, so she carried that burden alone. Even extended family didn't know, but a few days before her mom died, she decided that she wanted to see her brother. Completely unaware up until this point that his sister was dying from cancer, her brother flew out, and they were able to spend her last days together. Looking back on this loss, she is able to see how God truly gives you the knowledge that it's your time to go, that He's coming to bring you home. Her mother was at peace when she passed. Difficult as it was to let her mother go, she was able to see how God brought good from it. God was at work in the lives of those around her even through this tragedy.

Her father lived for another 10 years before developing lymphoma, and they only gave him six months to live. As she thinks back to this time, she can remember how amazing her father was through all of this. He never complained once about his illness or his diagnosis. He moved in with them, and he continued to attend church with them every week. He enjoyed being with his family. He lived life well to the end. But watching her father's health slowly decline was one of the biggest tests of her faith thus far. She was an only child. She had already lost one parent. How could God possibly ask her to now let him go too, all she had left? She remembers the final days of his life through tears. Their pastor came along with another friend to pray for him. Her friend told her that she needed to let him go, that she needed to tell him, "You can go." She knew she needed to, but it was the last thing she wanted to do, the hardest three words she would ever have to say. Saying those words, though, released her father back to the Lord. They had a few more days to spend together, sharing stories, and growing close to each other even in the end. She learned more about him in those final few days than she felt that she knew before. She listened to stories that she had never heard. Those final days were so precious, so treasured.

Although confident that her father was now with the Lord and no longer suffering, she couldn't help but feel so alone. Grief overwhelmed her. Who was going to be there for her now? She fell into a depression, slipping further and further away from God and her faith. She began drinking to numb the pain. She couldn't sleep at night, so she slept during the day. It was a relentless downward spiral. In the midst of this overwhelming darkness, a close girlfriend encouraged her to seek help. She needed a support group, people who would understand what she was going through.

The group was comprised of a mix of people who had lost someone in their lives, but mostly those who had lost a spouse. There was a man there who looked just like her dad, making it almost impossible for her to stay...but she did. Over the weeks that she attended this group, what really struck her was hearing the stories of these people who had lost the loves of their lives. Many had been married for 50-60 years, leaving them with such an incredible void in their hearts over the loss of their spouse. Listening to them share allowed her to see that she never thought in those ten years how much her dad must have missed her mom. They had such a loving marriage, and she never acknowledged the pain he must have been in. He was always so optimistic. That showed her that she had hit rock bottom. She knew she had to look up, and when she did, God was reaching out to her.

Her mom was a really strong person, but she never saw it in herself. She went through so much hardship, but her strength was rooted in her faith in God and her time in His Word. As she reflected on the life of her mom, something changed inside her own heart. Why wasn't she relying on God like she had seen both of her parents do? It took awhile, but through the love and support of her friends, family, and her pastor, she was finally able to see that she was God's child. She was just on loan to her earthly parents, but ultimately, God wanted her to see that He was her Father. Feeling like an orphan in this world but finally seeing that she was adopted by her Heavenly Father allowed faith and freedom to flood her heart. God had blessed her with so many friends during this time, and although they didn't share the same blood, they shared the same Father.

One might think this is where Her Story ends, but God wasn't through with her yet. Despite having faced the loss of both of her parents, trials would continue to penetrate her life at every turn, proving her faith genuine and causing her to learn what it means to fully rely on the Lord. Her life was flooded with numerous health issues, surgeries, and regular hospitalizations. She had several knee surgeries leading to both knee replacements, a hysterectomy, kidney stones that sent her to the hospital taking three months to heal, and she was diagnosed with lupus and diabetes. Then, when it seemed like things couldn't get much worse for her, she contracted MRCA. The doctors feared that it would spread to a vital organ, so she was immediately hospitalized and forced to undergo more tests, scans, and medications than she thought humanly possible. She remembers the fear she felt and wondering if she was ever going to make it through this. Sometimes she wondered if she would ever leave that hospital. She almost lost her life in this fight, but every day, God met her with His presence and gave her strength. She faced a long road of physical therapy and intense pain, but she emerged from that fight realizing that it was nothing that she did to make it out on the other side. It was God's hand of mercy and grace that pulled her through. She never stopped trusting in the Lord. He had already brought her through too much for her to walk away now. Convinced that God was not through with her yet, she clung to her faith in Him. She didn't know His plan, but she trusted His plan. The unknown can be frustrating, but she wouldn't be afraid of it.

Finally on the road to recovery, she was given the opportunity to take over the prayer chain at her church. People would submit prayer requests, and she would reply to them with Scripture verses and words of encouragement. She poured over God's Word for the three months that she led this prayer chain, unaware of how God was using this time to prepare her heart for what would come next. The last day of her physical therapy from her MRCA recovery, she came home to a prayer request from a woman at her church whom had just been diagnosed with stage 4 breast cancer. She immediately began searching through the Bible to find verses to encourage this woman when the phone rang. It was her doctor calling with the results from her recent mammogram. "You flunked your mammogram." What timing? And what a delivery?! They told her that she needed to find a surgeon right away. So, she hung up and called her daughter right away. "Pam, I think I have breast cancer." Her daughter, always the voice of reason, encouraged her not to worry but to trust in the Lord. Despite this new blow, her response was one of faith. She was going to do everything she could and leave the rest up to God. She went through chemotherapy for six months, ending in a double mastectomy the following September. Although this was an extremely difficult end, she really was in a good place. She wasn't even shaken. Most people were mad for her, but she was so steady in her faith. Her response was always, "I will take as much as God gives me." God had lovingly prepared her for this trial through her prayer chain. She was daily devouring God's Word, in hopes of offering encouragement to others who were struggling, but it was that time in His Word that God used to give her the strength to make it through this too. As she battled the cancer, God would remind her of the promises in His Word that she had dug out to share with others:

"But from there you will seek the LORD your God and you will find Him, if you search after Him with all your heart and with all your soul."

—Deuteronomy 4:29

"Rejoice in hope, be patient in tribulation, be constant in prayer."

—Romans 12:12

Her unwavering faith would almost offend people at times, but she had already faced death 3 times just through the MRCA, and God continued to see her safely through. She trusted God's hand. The hardest part was after her mastectomy. She had to take off the bandage, and see herself for the 1st time. She was not prepared for that, how could she be? She looked at her scars and said to God, "This isn't how you made me, but this is how I am." At that moment, she thought back to her mom and how she must have felt after going through the very same thing. She realized that God had chosen them to be her parents in a grand plan that started long before she was even thought of. Her mom had shown her what faith looked like. Her mom had taught her the power of prayer and the love of Christian community. They weren't even biologically related, but she experienced the same things her mom had. If her mom could do all that by the grace of God, so could she. In the midst of this storm, blessings flooded her way. How could she complain about her plight when God continued to bless her through it? She was surrounded by a loving and supportive family. She was covered in constant prayer, perhaps the greatest blessing of all.

All of this, and she has still had several scares since her cancer. She contracted another severe infection that almost resulted in losing her leg, but her faith remained. Her response: "If I lose my leg, I'm going to have a heck of a shoe sale!" She meets each challenge with her resilient faith in the God who saves. Every illness, every surgery, every scar is a reminder of where she has been with the Lord. Just as Jacob wrestled with the Lord and walked away with a limp to remind him, she has numerous physical reminders of God's grace on her life and what He has brought her through. It's the standing joke in her family, "How long can mom go without being in the hospital?" 2011 was hospital free! January 2012 led her back into the hospital with a mini-stroke. Yet, she awakes each day to God's mercies that are new. She trusts in the Lord. Each trial has confirmed that He is all-powerful, and that He is in control. He is the Great Physician, and her life is in His hands. She will never stop praying. She trusts that this is part of His plan and so is the outcome. She seeks to glorify Him in between by sharing her story – her story of resilient faith in a faithful God. She swore she wouldn't live past thirty. She will be sixty this year. If life was always smooth, we could never grow into the person God wants us to be. There were times when she thought she must have the worst luck in the world, times when she wrote goodbye letters to her family and friends, but now she sees how God was pursuing her through it all. "If we have faith, we don't have to worry. If we worry, we must not have faith." She won't question God anymore. Her faith will not be shaken!

Sitting across the room from her, listening to her share Her Story, I was moved to tears. The faith she possesses could only come through much refining in the fire of adversity, yet her faith remains through each and every trial. She is a treasure! Her presence is a blessing to everyone she comes in contact with because her faith is contagious. She exudes faith. She models it. She is Linda Hartig, and I am blessed to call her my sister in Christ.

Your Story

There is something so significant about our faith story, or our conversion story. It's our spiritual birthday. What is your faith story? Write out the details and events surrounding your conversion—how and when you came to faith in Jesus Christ. Write out your faith story.

WALKING IN HIS WAYS—OBEDIENCE

Genesis 22

1. Obedience requires _____, _____,

   and _____ to the God whose ways are higher than our own.

   (verses 1-3)

2. At the heart of obedience, there is an _____ that God

   is _____ and _____ in _____ that He does. (verses 4-10)

3. The _____ of the Lord is experienced as a _____ of

   _____. (verses 11-19)

Week Five *Teaching Outline*

Discussion Questions

1. What was the most significant time of devotion in your homework this week?

2. In what ways do you see active obedience to God and His Word displayed in your life?

3. Are there any areas in your life that are lacking the joy of the Lord?

4. Is there an area of disobedience in your life that God is calling you out of tonight?

5. Are you ready to start obeying God's Word tonight? Are you willing? Will you surrender?

Week Five

WALKING IN HIS WAYS— OBEDIENCE

THIS WEEK'S MEMORY VERSE

"The LORD will establish you as His holy people, as He promised you on oath, if you keep the commands of the LORD your God and walk in His ways."

—Deuteronomy 28:9

Day One
WALKING IN HIS WAYS—OBEDIENCE

• • • • • • • • • • •

Day Two
A PRAYER OF OBEDIENCE

• • • • • • • • • • •

Day Three
OBEDIENCE WHEN IT'S HARD

• • • • • • • • • • •

Day Four
OBEDIENCE IN PRAYER

• • • • • • • • • • •

Day Five
HER STORY

Day One
WALKING IN HIS WAYS—OBEDIENCE

Over the past few weeks, we've struggled through brokenness and surrender. We've wrestled with trust and faith. Today, we will seek to stand upon our faith and move to obedience. Today begins Obedience Week. It's the next step we'll take together as we strive to be women found on our knees at the feet of our Savior. I hope you are enjoying this journey. We have tackled some difficult issues and been forced to face some painful things, but I pray that as you move from brokenness to surrender, from trust to faith, that God is revealing Himself to you along the way, engulfing you in His presence, and pouring out His matchless love upon you. Being a Christ follower is a high calling, one that requires we represent Him well. Obedience is key in this. Join me as we dive into the riches of God's Word and together seek to walk in His ways.

Walking in obedience may be a phrase that you've heard often in the church. Or perhaps you aren't so acquainted with these words. Either way, I think it's a phrase that needs to have some light shed on it. What does it really mean to walk in obedience? What does obedience look like lived out? I was just as curious as you probably are, so I began to search through God's Word to find some clarity, the greatest source of truth. I did a simple word search for the word "walk". Now, I don't know about you, but I love to study God's Word. Give me several hours, a big table strewn with books, commentaries, the Bible, something to write with, and a large cup of coffee and you will find a very happy Cherie. I just love the treasures I find as I dig into His Word. I come thirsty, and the water I receive satisfies. It's an amazing thing. There were numerous verses that came up by just searching for the word "walk", but what I found to be most interesting was that the word "walk" was often found within the phrase "walk in His ways". What's even more fascinating is that several of these verses were found in the book of Deuteronomy alone. Let me just list a few of them for you. Grab your Bible, and let's do a little Bible study, shall we?

"Walk in all the way that the LORD your God has commanded you, so that you may live and prosper and prolong your days in the land that you will possess." —Deuteronomy 5:33

"And now, O Israel, what does the LORD your God ask of you but to fear the LORD your God, to walk in all His ways, to love Him, to serve the LORD your God with all your heart and with all your soul." —Deuteronomy 10:12

"You have declared this day that the LORD is your God and that you will walk in His ways, that you will keep His decrees, commands and laws, and that you will obey Him." —Deuteronomy 26:17

"The LORD will establish you as His holy people, as He promised you on oath, if you keep the commands of the LORD your God and walk in His ways." —Deuteronomy 28:9

"For I command you today to love the LORD your God, to walk in His ways, and to keep His commands, decrees and laws; then you will live and increase, and the LORD your God will bless you in the land you are entering to possess." —Deuteronomy 30:16

Over and over again we see the phrase "walk in His ways". It is important to notice that each time, the phrase is imperative. This is a command, not a suggestion. To be quite honest, I don't think that God offers us many suggestions in His Word. He says, and we do; end of discussion. He requires our obedience. Anything less is sin. It is His desire that we walk as He walked, do as He did, speak as He spoke, and love as He loved. He calls us to obedience.

We can see that this is a very serious issue, one that we must get a grasp on. Walk in his ways. So, what are His ways? The good news is that God didn't leave us empty-handed. Throughout the Bible we can see God's ways demonstrated, especially through the life of Christ in the four gospels. In complete perfection, Jesus Christ displayed justice, love, mercy, and humility among numerous other characteristics as He walked the face of this earth. He is our model. We are to imitate Him. We are to walk in His ways. Obedience to God's Word is key for every Christ follower. We must read His Word, abide by it, meditate on it, stand upon it, and live it. That is what it means to walk in His ways.

There was a particular season in my own life when the LORD called me to obedience, and I found it difficult to walk in His ways. Perhaps you can relate. It was easy for me to talk the talk, but when it came down to walking the walk, well that was a different story. I knew I was supposed to trust the LORD, knowing that wherever He would lead me He would also go with me and that I would not ever be left alone without His presence. Still, it was hard to take that first step of obedience, not being able to see what was ahead. As I chose to walk in obedience and go where He was calling me to go, yes, there was pain as I had to let go of all that I had been holding on to, but even more so I was reminded of His blessing that always follows obedience. When we choose to walk in His ways and be obedient to His Word, blessing naturally follows. That is just His way. He is a good God, and out of His love He chooses to bless obedience.

What does this look like for you right now in your life? What particular obedience might the LORD be calling you to? Might I encourage you again, dear sister, to walk in His ways. The LORD will bless your obedience.

"He has showed you, O man, what is good. And what does the LORD require of you? To act justly and to love mercy and to walk humbly with your God."

—Micah 6:8

I. Are you one that struggles with obedience? Do you find it difficult to obey?

2. How have you seen past disobediences bring suffering into your life?

3. What is one area of disobedience in your life that you can turn from and commit to the Lord today?

< 95 >

4. *Journal a prayer of commitment to the Lord, offering Him the past and choosing to obey Him with your present and your future.*

Day Two
A PRAYER OF OBEDIENCE

"Trust in the Lord, and do good; dwell in the land and befriend faithfulness. Delight yourself in the Lord, and He will give you the desires of your heart. Commit your way to the Lord; trust in Him, and He will act. He will bring forth your righteousness as the light, and your justice as the noonday. Be still before the Lord and wait patiently for Him."

—Psalm 37:3-7a

Heavenly Father,

I'm tired of running from you. I'm done resisting you and your ways. I'm weary from my disobedience. Today, Lord, I choose obedience. Today I choose to trust you and to do good. Your Word calls me to obedience. Your command to me is that I would walk in your ways and follow your instruction for my life. Forgive me for holding man's wisdom and understanding above the authority of God's Word. For far too long, I've reasoned my way through life, refusing to change and resisting the conviction of your Holy Spirit. Today, I choose to place myself fully under the authority of your Word.

Your Word tells me that when I choose to delight in you that you will give me the desires of my heart. Help me to understand the meaning of this promise, that when I'm delighting in you and your Word, you change the desires of my heart to match yours. When my heart is beating in accordance with yours, it is then that I find complete joy. So, today, I choose obedience. I choose to delight in you and not in the fading and fleeting things of this world. Today, I choose you first. I will run to you first in obedience, and I will seek satisfaction in you alone. You, Lord, can fill my cup. You alone can satisfy the desires of my heart. So, in obedience, I choose to delight in you today.

Father, too many times, I've taken matters into my own hands. I've made a destructive pattern of trying to "handle things" on my own without consulting you. Today, I choose obedience. Today, I commit all my ways to you and surrender the control. I desire that you order my steps and direct me in the way I should go. From today forward, teach me to commit my every way to you, Lord.

Lord, I want to rest in you and your unchanging character. Help me to be still before you and to wait patiently for you. You will show up. You will speak. You will act. All you require of me is my obedience to you in the waiting. Part of that obedience is being still. I struggle with this so much, Lord, but I'm tired of striving. I'm tired of wrestling with you over this. Teach me to choose obedience in this, too. Today, Lord, I choose obedience.

In Jesus' name,
Amen

< **97** >

1. *In reading the previous passage, has God convicted you of a specific area of disobedience in your life?*

2. *Journal a prayer of response to the Lord using Psalm 37:3-7a, as I've done above. Commit to obedience today.*

Day Three

OBEDIENCE WHEN IT'S HARD

"Why are you downcast, O my soul? Why so disturbed within me? Put your hope in God, for I will yet praise Him, my Savior and my God."

—Psalm 42:5

Do you ever feel just like that—down, discouraged, and tired of the struggle, but telling yourself at the same time what you know to be true? "Put your hope in God." Sometimes it's nothing more than a rehearsed and a learned response for some, the right thing to do. Not that obedience is ever easy, but there are certainly times when it's harder than others, times when running in the opposite direction seems far easier than obedience, yet God calls us to a life of obedience and to live in obedience to His Word...always, no matter what. But what about the times when it's really hard to obey?

Psalm 42 seems to have a lot to say about that difficult question. Join me there, and take a moment to read through it in its entirety...

The writer of this Psalm expresses throughout a desperation and anguish of his soul. Life is just not easy for him right now. Trouble seems to come at him from every angle, and in his struggle to find meaning in his pain, he wrestles with God and poses many questions. What utterly astounds me, though, is how he repeatedly brings his focus back to his greatest need...God. Although many of his needs seemingly go unmet, he understands that it is God and God alone that will quench his parched soul. The beauty of verse one captivates me every time I read it:

"As the deer pants for streams of water, so my soul pants for you, O God."

Have you ever craved God that much? Have you ever been virtually dehydrated for His touch and thirsty for His presence in your life? If you haven't, perhaps your prayer should be one of repentance: "Father, forgive me for being far too satisfied with so little of your presence." Obedience when it's hard is running to God in the middle of your desperation as opposed to running from Him in your self-sufficiency. Although the Psalmist recounts with sorrow the wonderful places he has been and longs to return to (verse 4), he immediately follows this with the reminder to put his hope in God, not in his past. Isn't it such a tendency of ours to wish back to the good times, to the places we once were and think how much greener the grass is

< 99 >

on the other side? The grass is green where you water it. Remember that, and be reminded by Psalm 42 that our hope must rest in God alone. It is when we choose to place our hope in God that obedience follows. Notice in verse 5 the questions that are immediately followed by committed obedience despite the circumstances.

"For I will yet praise Him, my Savior and my God."

Obedience chooses to act on faith as opposed to feelings. The feelings of the Psalmist at this point are discouragement and despair. However, by faith he defaults to obedience. He chose to praise God in his storm. He chose to remember the Lord in his struggle (verse 6). He chose to meditate on God's love that is with him always (verse 8). He chose obedience, even when it was hard.

One of my favorite Christian artists, Kari Jobe, released a new album recently, and I've been so blessed by my times of worship while listening to it. One song in particular speaks to my heart in regards to this theme of obedience. It's titled "Steady My Heart." Here are just a few of the lyrics:

Wish it could be easy
Why is life so messy
Why is pain a part of us
There are days I feel like
Nothing ever goes right
Sometimes it just hurts so much

But You're here
You're real
I know I can trust You

Even when it hurts
Even when it's hard
Even when it all just falls apart
I will run to You
Cause I know that You are
Lover of my soul
Healer of my scars
You steady my heart

Perhaps Psalm 42 is the reminder that we need today...obedience, even when it's hard, is the choice we must make. He will steady your heart. Run to Him.

1. What difficult obedience is God calling you to right now? Why is it hard for you to obey Him in this?

2. In response to Psalm 42, journal a prayer to God asking Him to help you to respond to all situations with obedience.

Day Four
OBEDIENCE IN PRAYER

"And pray in the Spirit on all occasions with all kinds of prayers and requests. With this in mind, be alert and always keep on praying for all the saints."

—Ephesians 6:18

One of the things that I find so refreshing when I read Scripture is coming across a verse or a passage that is easy to understand. You know what I mean, right? When I read "Children, obey your parents..." in Ephesians 6:1, I get it. I know what it's saying. I understand the command there. When I read "Be imitators of God..." in Ephesians 5:1, I know that it's telling me to act as Jesus did. It's not a difficult command to understand. It's incredibly refreshing to come across such clear instruction in God's Word, isn't it? Our small group just decided to read through the Bible in a year together, and I have to admit that there are portions of Scripture that are difficult for me to understand. These portions are no less important nor are they any less inspired or true, but there are sections of God's Word that I have to wrestle through and ask the Lord to give me revelation and understanding as I read.

The beauty of our verse today is that it is clear in its instruction, and it is not difficult to understand.

"And pray in the Spirit on all occasions with all kinds of prayers and requests. With this in mind, be alert and always keep on praying for all the saints."

—Ephesians 6:18

It's the choice to DO IT that we find difficult. The Bible instructs us again in regards to prayer in 1 Thessalonians 5:17 with a short but simple command: "Pray continually." What is God's Word trying to tell us about prayer? What are we to learn about this discipline called prayer? I don't know about you, but when it comes to obedience, I prefer to use God's Word as my instruction manual. However, it is far too often that we find ourselves rationalizing our decisions away with excuses and human reasoning or justifying our behavior by the standards of this world. How about today we choose to obey God's Word and hold His Word up as our highest authority? Are you willing to do that? I pray that each of us finds ourselves choosing obedience today.

God's Word offers us some clear and important instruction when it comes to prayer. First and foremost, God commands us to pray. Prayer is not an option for the believer. So, how do we approach this thing called prayer? How do we walk in obedience to God's Word when it comes to prayer?

Pray regularly. Several scriptures speak directly to this instruction. Not only Ephesians 6:18 and 1 Thessalonians 5:17, but we are given Jesus Christ as our perfect example of consistent and regular prayer. The night He was betrayed into the hands of those who would crucify Him, He was found on His knees crying out to God the Father in prayer, praying the same prayer three times: "Take this cup from me. Yet not what I will, but what you will." (Mark 14:36) There was earnestness and consistency displayed in how Jesus prayed, and He calls us to be like Him.

Pray together. In addition to prayer being a regular and consistent practice in our own personal lives, the Bible also instructs us to make it a habit to pray with one another. In Acts 1:14, we see obedience in the lives of the disciples and other followers of Jesus in their joining together in prayer. "They all joined together constantly in prayer, along with the women and Mary the mother of Jesus, and with his brothers." They had the wisdom to see the importance and the necessity of regular times of prayer together. We should do the same. Regular fellowship and prayer with our brothers and sisters in Christ serves to strengthen our own faith in Jesus. We were never meant to live the Christian life alone.

Pray for others. Ephesians 6:18 not only instructs us to pray consistently, but also to pray for fellow believers, or "saints". As Christians, we are called to the lifestyle of prayer, and part of that is not only being aware of others needs but also lifting up those needs to our Father in prayer. Are you one who is found on your knees in prayer for the body of Christ? It's so easy for us to say, "I'll be praying for you", but do we actually pray? Often times, I'll say that and then walk away, completely forgetting to pray, failing to fulfill the commitment that I just made. A few years ago, I began to form a habit in my prayer life that has proven to be such a blessing. When someone comes to me sharing a need with me, instead of saying "I'll pray for you", I have begun to say, "Can I pray for you right now?" Pray in the moment. Stop and pray right there. Be a blessing to others by not only praying for them, but by praying with them.

1. God calls us to a lifestyle of prayer. How can you discipline your day to make prayer more of a priority? How can you begin to include prayer into your schedule regularly?

2. *Who do you pray with? Is it your spouse? Your accountability partner? Your small group or Bible study?*

3. *What does your prayer list consist of? Are you currently praying for anyone? Spend some time right now and journal a prayer for someone in your life that has shared a need with you. Pray for them and let them know that you are praying for them right now.*

Day Five
HER STORY

"For this reason, because I have heard of your faith in the Lord Jesus and your love toward all the saints, I do not cease to give thanks for you, remembering you in my prayers, that the God of our Lord Jesus Christ, the Father of glory, may give you a spirit of wisdom and of revelation in the knowledge of Him, having the eyes of your hearts enlightened, that you may know what is the hope to which He has called you..."

—Ephesians 1:15-18a

There are some stories that move me to tears. Some that cause my heart to overflow with joy and praise to the Lord for all that He has done. Some stories cause my heart to ache and bring me to my knees in prayer, desperate to see God move on behalf of one's life. Most stories of God's mighty work take years to shape, and it's in the waiting that beauty is formed. It's in the desert seasons that God strips away the chaff, and creates something in us far more beautiful than before. Her story today captures all of the above. Her story is one that ushers me into the presence of the Lord in praise and adoration for all that He has done to redeem one life from the pit. Her story has the potential to change you forever as you witness God's hand at work in her life. Her story changed me. This is her story...

Her story began tragically. When she was just nine days old, her father was brutally murdered. Growing up without knowing the love of a father, her childhood years were spent envious of other girls who attended Daddy Daughter dances and received love, protection, and attention from their fathers. She longed to have someone to call "Dad". There was a void inside that she couldn't seem to fill, an aching emptiness. This longing for love that wasn't being met grew over time. The pain was so intense that it drove her to extreme measures to fill the void within. In hopes of easing her pain, she relentlessly pursued anything and everything that she thought would bring her happiness – destructive relationships, affirmation, and people pleasing among other things. Despite the fact that these pursuits only brought momentary relief from the storm raging inside of her, she continued to seek comfort in them.

Yet because the Lord rises to show us compassion and never ceases to pursue us with His steadfast love, God divinely placed a group of people in her life when she was a teenager who told her how much God loved her and wanted to be the father she never had. The words almost sounded too good to be true! Oh, how she wanted to know the love of a father! But sadly, even though she "prayed the prayer" to invite Christ into her heart at the age of 18, she went on to live many more years of a fruitless and defeated Christian life. Although she did believe that she had a Savior and wanted to grow in her walk with the Lord, she was neither equipped nor eager to make Jesus the Lord of her life. Selfishness, compromise, defeat, and sin-confess cycles still consumed her life and kept her from knowing the abundant life in Jesus Christ. There was no growth, no fruit, and no lasting change. Nothing in her life set her apart from the world. Her attempts at appearing holy were stained with the guilt of hidden sins, and her life was full of secrecy and shame. She longed to be like those Christian women she saw at church who seemed so in love with Jesus, but she didn't know how. She was stuck in a life of sin and complacency. Keeping one foot on each side of the fence, her Christian life was at best lukewarm. She knew she needed God's love and even wanted it, but she wasn't ready to be "all in" and live for Him alone. The sacrifice appeared to be too great.

You might say she had forgotten God, but God had not forgotten her. One divinely appointed day seven years later at church, she sat through the very sermon she needed to hear most called "Turning the Tide on Sin" based on Psalm 51. God's Word became alive to her in those moments, and it was as if the words from that passage leapt off the page and pierced her heart, just the sort of thing that God's Word tends to do. The verses within the Psalm accurately described her spiritual condition. She was in desperate need of God's mercy. She recognized that she needed to be washed and cleansed from her sin. The Holy Spirit stepped in and brought a true conviction of sin, not guilt or shame, but a godly sorrow. She'll never forget that day, the day that God gave sight to her spiritual blindness and ministered directly to her heart. For the first time, she was able to see the difference between true repentance versus feeling sorry and condemned for her sin. She had a new perspective. She was finally able to see how her sin grieved the heart of God, and that changed everything. She found God that day, broken and unsure of how to pick up the pieces, but she knew that she needed the victory that was available to her. Through Christ's death and resurrection, she would overcome the grip of sin and shame on her life. That day, her life changed forever. That day, she surrendered every area of her life to the Lordship of Jesus Christ, refusing to turn back to her old ways, and committing to a life in pursuit of Christ. Her new life in Christ was far better, but certainly not easy. The walking out of her repentance began a two-year journey of confessing her secret sins that bound her in shame for so long. It was a trembling step of faith that she took to seek restoration with others that her sins had wounded. With the prayerful support of a Bible teacher and mentor, she walked through one of the most difficult seasons of her life toward freedom with God by her side and His strength within her, leading her every step of the way. And because God is good and does abundantly more than we could ask or even imagine, He also brought a new friend into her life who prayed with and for her, taught her about God's Word, and held her accountable to being the godly woman Christ was calling her to be.

The Lord carried her through this trying and difficult season, growing her each day as she chose to follow Him in obedience no matter the cost. Countless hours spent in prayer and in the Word have changed her from the inside out. It's been beyond incredible to see first-hand how God has mercifully brought "times of refreshing" (Acts 3:19) to her soul. She has been set free from the lies she believed for so long, and she now walks in truth. What Satan intended for evil, God meant for good in her life. He healed and restored her marriage of twelve years. For the first time, her identity in Christ is secure, and she daily lives on the promise that she is a new creation in Christ and has an eternal assurance in Him. Now, she is that woman who loves the Lord, a wife, a mother, a woman of noble character! Because she has seen first hand what God can do to restore a broken, empty heart, she now has an insatiable desire to minister to other women who find themselves in the pit that she once resided in. Every opportunity that God gives her, she shares her story to point other women to the awesome Healer, Redeemer, and Restorer, Jesus Christ.

What I love about her story is that she points all the praise, honor, and glory to Christ, because He deserves it. Her story compels me to love Jesus more. Her story is filled with the truths of God's rich mercy and grace. She is my best friend, my sister in Christ, my accountability partner, a devoted member of my prayer team, and a blessing that is far too difficult to capture into words. I'm following harder after Jesus because of her presence in my life. Ivette, thank you for loving Jesus like you do, and thank you for sharing your story. You're an agent of His truth and grace. You radiate God's love to all whom you encounter. I am a life that was changed because of your faithful obedience. I love you.

Your Story

How has walking in His ways in obedience been an active theme in your life? What obediences have marked your life and drawn you closer to Christ? Write out your story of obedience.

....
....
....
....
....
....
....
....
....
....
....
....
....
....
....
....
....
....
....
....
....
....
....
....
....
....

RIVERS IN THE DESERT—BLESSING

Isaiah 58

1. The _____ of disobedience is forfeited _____.
   (verses 1-5)

2. First _____, then... (verses 6-7, 9b-10a, and 13)

3. The experienced _____ of obedience is _____.
   (verses 8-9a, 10b-12, and 14)

Discussion Questions

1. What was the most significant time of devotion in your homework this week?

2. Is there an area of disobedience in your life that God is calling you out of today?

3. God's promises in Isaiah 58 are conditional upon what factor? How about in 1 John 1:9?

4. How has God opened up your eyes to His blessings in your life? Have His blessings come in unexpected ways?

5. Verse 14 ends with such a strong declaration: "The mouth of the LORD has spoken." How has this truth brought comfort and confidence to your current situation?

Week Six

RIVERS IN THE DESERT —BLESSING

THIS WEEK'S MEMORY VERSE

"The LORD will guide you always; He will satisfy your needs in a sun-scorched land and will strengthen your frame. You will be like a well-watered garden, like a spring whose waters never fail."

—Isaiah 58:11

Day One
RIVERS IN THE DESERT—BLESSING

· · · · · · · · · ·

Day Two
A PRAYER OF BLESSING FOR YOU

· · · · · · · · · ·

Day Three
THE PROMISE-GIVER

· · · · · · · · · ·

Day Four
BLESSED ARE...

· · · · · · · · · ·

Day Five
HER STORY

Day One
RIVERS IN THE DESERT—BLESSING

"Behold, I am doing a new thing; now it springs forth, do you not perceive it? I will make a way in the wilderness and rivers in the desert."

—Isaiah 43:19

There's nothing like coming across water in the desert, is there? I live in Phoenix, Arizona, so desert conditions are something that I'm very familiar with. Dreadfully hot temperatures characterize close to half of the year here, and without drinking a consistent amount of water, one cannot survive. I remember a few years ago when I was in Egypt how incredible water tasted after a long, hot day. We spent a majority of our time there prayer walking through different parts of Cairo, and the temperatures were very warm. Water seemed to be the only beverage I ever craved during our stay there. We even took a trip down into the Sahara Desert to an oasis a few hours from the city. Sand and wasteland was all you could see for miles. Water would have been a welcomed blessing to any traveler through those parts.

We have begun our final week of Bible study together, "Rivers in the Desert"...almost seems like an impossibility, or simply unfeasible, doesn't it? Yet, we read this phrase within the promise of this verse. God is doing a new thing, and now it springs forth! We've been on a journey together over the past five weeks, seeking to be women who are found on our knees at the feet of Jesus in passionate pursuit of Him. Have you begun to see that desire at work within you? We've been through brokenness and surrender together. We've embraced trust and faith and have come to an understanding of what it means to walk in His ways in obedience. Now we meet God at work, making a way in the wilderness and rivers in the desert. Have you ever felt like your life was a wilderness, a desert wasteland, dry and parched, desperately needing new life? "A way in the wilderness and rivers in the desert"...that's what God promises, and His promise is one of provision and blessing.

There have been many dry, desert-like seasons in my life. I'm certain you could say the same. Times like these are to be expected in our lives, yet we're never quite ready for them when they come, are we? Something that I've learned over the last several years as I've walked with the Lord is that He rarely seems to remove the "desert" from my life, although He is completely able to. Rather, He brings refreshing water to my desert, quenching my thirst and allowing me to continue on in His strength. You see, the desert you find yourself in right now might be a season that continues for some time. God knows the length of it down to the minute, and we can be assured that it won't be one minute too long. He controls the length and the intensity of each trial, each desert season. What His promise says though is that He will not leave us in the desert without water. "Rivers in the desert"...that is our blessing. Your desert season might not be removed, but you can be sure that Jesus will meet you in it. He'll meet you at the well. As we seek to follow Jesus Christ, fully surrendering our brokenness to Him, choosing to trust Him to be all that He says He is, placing our complete faith in Him, and walking in obedience to His Word, He faithfully pours out His blessings into our lives. His blessings here are the waters we need to go on, the sustenance we must have to finish the race well.

What desert do you find yourself in right now? Is it a lack of desire to spend time in His Word? Is it a painful season of heartache and loss? Are you grieving? Do you just need direction and guidance on where to go or what to do? Rest in His promise today. He makes a way in the wilderness. He places rivers in the desert to bring new life. He doesn't leave us alone, and He will never forsake us. He is true to His Word, and His promise endures. Come to the river, receive His blessings, and taste and see that the Lord is good.

1. Have you ever experienced God's blessings in dry seasons of your life? How?

2. *Journal a prayer of thanksgiving to the Lord, praising Him for His constant provision and presence in your life, even if the "desert" remains.*

Day Two
A PRAYER OF BLESSING FOR YOU

"The LORD bless you and keep you;
the LORD make His face to shine upon you
and be gracious to you;
The LORD lift up His countenance upon you
and give you peace."

—Numbers 6:24-26

I know that I've said this before, but I do pray over each lesson that I write. I pray that God will inspire my words to speak truth, life, and wisdom into the hearts of each and every reader. I pray for you when I write, asking that the LORD has prepared your heart for whatever it is that He wants to say to you. I pray each time that you are drawn closer to Jesus after spending time reading His Word. I pray that lives are forever changed for God's glory through my ministry.

Today is no different. I have been praying that God will sing His blessing over you through His Word as we pray together today. Today's lesson is my prayer for you, a prayer of blessing for you. I want each of you to know that you are loved by an awesome God, you are being pursued by His matchless love, and you are covered in prayer by His servant. May your hearts be encouraged today by His truth.

"The LORD bless you and keep you"

Heavenly Father,

I lift up my dear sisters to you today asking that you fulfill your promise to them and reveal your faithfulness to them today. I ask that you place your favor upon their lives, and that you bless them with every good blessing that comes from above. As they seek your face today, as they call out to you in prayer, hear their cries and answer them with your love and your presence. Draw them close to you and keep them by your side. May the nearness of your presence be the cry of their hearts.

"The LORD make His face to shine upon you"

Lord, your presence alone is the greatest blessing. Shine your face upon them, causing their faith to flourish and their doubt to fade. As you reveal more of yourself to them each day, create within them a deeper desire for more time spent in your presence. Your Word tells us that when we seek you, we will find you when we search for you with all of our heart. Lord, they've come today in search of you. Reveal the beauty of your face to each one as they passionately pursue after you.

"and be gracious to you"

Today, may they know the power of your grace in their lives. You extend mercy and grace towards them each new day. Cause them to live in that grace and to depend upon it. Continue to show them how wonderful you are and how deep your affections are for them. It is only because of your grace that we can come to you today.

"The LORD lift up His countenance upon you"

Again, I ask that you reveal the beauty of your face to them. For when they see the beauty of the LORD, their hearts will swell with faith. So, shine upon them today. Cause them to recognize your beauty all around them and to praise you for it.

"and give you peace."

Fill them with a peace today that surpasses all understanding, a peace that cannot be described or defined apart from you, Jesus. As you cover them in your peace, cause all the chaos and confusion in their lives to quiet in your presence and renew, restore, and rebuild them there. Bless them today, Lord Jesus, with your love, your presence, and your peace.

In Jesus' name,
Amen

1. *Journal your own prayer as I've done above using these verses. Pray God's Word today over your family.*

2. *What encouragement have you received from this prayer from God's Word? Journal your response of gratitude to the Lord for His blessings.*

Day Three
THE PROMISE-GIVER

"Remember not the former things, nor consider the things of old. Behold, I am doing a new thing; now it springs forth, do you not perceive it? I will make a way in the wilderness and rivers in the desert."
—Isaiah 43:18-19

If there is one thing I have learned about the character of God as I have studied His Word it is that He makes promises to His children, and He keeps His promises. As I look back over the years of my life, it becomes increasingly easy for me to see how, when, and where God has been faithful to keep His promises. Although I have gone through numerous seasons of pain, trial, and hardship, He has never once forsaken me, just as He said He never would. As I reflect on the times of need in my life, I can see so clearly how He was my Provider. When I remember the times that my heart was breaking as I grieved the loss of loved ones, the LORD drew near to me when I could do nothing but weep against His chest. He held me in His arms, and He comforted me with His Spirit.

There are an incredible amount of promises in God's Word, so many so that our faith should be sparked to life by just the knowledge of it. Today, I want to return our focus to one such promise found in the treasure of Isaiah 43:18-19. Grab your Bible, and let's dive in together, shall we? I like to underline portions of Scripture that God uses to propel my faith forward. As I flip through the pages of my Bible, the underlined portions serve as a reminder to me of where Jesus and I have been together. Perhaps you like to do the same. In my Bible, next to these two verses, I have written "Arizona". Maybe because the verses reference wilderness and desert, I felt so inclined to remind myself of my physical environment. There is a deeper meaning though to be grasped. These two short verses begin with a command: "Forget the past, stop dwelling on it!" Of course, that is my paraphrase, but how important it is to grasp this here. We far too often get stuck in a rut of what once was. Whether we look back longingly, wishing we were where we once were, or we reflect back regretfully, filled with shame and guilt. Neither is the response that God would want from us. Because of His amazing grace, He's forgiven and forgotten our pasts. Why can't we move on from them and settle into the riches of His mercy and grace? Because we are human, because we are weak and frail, we need constant reminders from His Word. So, we now find ourselves at verse 19 – He is at work right now in your life, and He is doing a new thing! Whether you find yourself in the pasture of His blessing or in the wilderness right now, He makes us a significant promise in this verse. He will make a way, and He'll provide rivers in the desert to satisfy our parched souls. His promises are His blessings to us. Today, right now, wherever you are, choose to fall back on the promises of God. Default to faith in His Word rather than doubt. He makes promises, and He is faithful to keep them.

I'd like to invite you to respond right now to the Lord. Spend some time reflecting on the truth in His Word. Let's go deeper with Him.

1. What is one of your favorite promises in the Bible? Find the verse, write it down, and commit it to memory this week. Then journal a response of praise to God for making that promise to you.

2. **Do you ever find yourself doubting the promises of God? Be honest with yourself and with the Lord. He knows already anyway. Doubt is an enemy of faith. Journal a confession to the Lord of any area in your life that you have doubted Him, and ask Him to increase your faith to believe that He will do what He says He will do.**

3. **Read through Isaiah 43 in its entirety, and list every promise you come across in this chapter. Finish with a prayer of thanksgiving for all that God has promised.**

Day Four
BLESSED ARE...

"Blessed are those who hunger and thirst for righteousness, for they shall be satisfied."
—Matthew 5:6

As I briefly mentioned before, a few years ago, I had the privilege of going to Egypt on a short-term missions trip through my church. The trip was filled with incredible moments and countless stories that could be shared, but one of the things that stands out to me the most from my time there was the passage of Scripture that we studied as a team each day. We read through Matthew 5, the beginning of the Sermon on the Mount. My heart was transformed each morning as we met to have our time of prayer and devotions, and I've been drawn back to this passage regularly since. The above verse in particular has had a tremendous impact on my understanding of faith. I want to share with you some of the things that God has laid on my heart, some of the truths that He has impressed in my mind, and some of the practical ways that I've been able to apply these convictions.

There are some questions that I wrestled with as I really took the time to study this verse. What does it look like to live a blessed life? I mean, the kind of blessing that God extends from His hand that transforms our lives in such a way that we find contentment? I'm not referring to happiness – an emotion that is often dependent upon outward circumstances. I'm not suggesting material blessing either. "Blessed" here is referring to a spiritual joy that is known by those who share in the salvation that only Jesus Christ can offer. Do I know this kind of blessing? Do you? This is a joy that can be had amidst difficulty. It's a lasting joy, a fullness, and it's what God intends for His children. How can I have this kind of blessed life that this verse speaks of? True blessing and satisfaction is granted to those who hunger and thirst for righteousness.

The words in this verse on their own are not difficult to understand. Yet when put together, they have profound impact. Allow me to elaborate. The word "hunger" for instance means a strong or compelling desire or craving, the painful sensation or state of weakness caused by the need of food. Thirst has a similar definition: a strong or eager desire or craving caused by the need of liquid. Hunger and thirst are not things I think about often, probably because I'm never truly desperate for food or water. They are needs that are immediately met whenever they arise.

It's interesting though how this verse was brought back to my mind just a few weeks ago. My husband and I spent a weekend away up at his family's cabin in the mountains. It's a beautifully peaceful place of retreat for us, and we love every opportunity we get to spend time there. If you know me at all, you know that I'm not much of a wilderness girl. I'm most comfortable in the noise and chaos of a bustling city, but I'm willing to step out of my comfort zone when my man is involved. He loves the outdoors—hiking, camping, fishing, etc. So, I took this opportunity to fill his love tank and agreed to go on a "short" hike with him through the woods. It was a gorgeous day with temperatures in the 70s. Since we only planned to be gone for about 30-45 minutes, we thought one water bottle each would suffice. Well, along the way we decided to be ambitious and take the trail we were hiking until it ended. We didn't realize that it was about five miles to the end, totaling a ten mile round trip hike! Needless to say, thirst became an issue. We finished both of our water bottles with miles left to hike. I was so thirsty. My fingers started to swell to the point that I couldn't move my wedding ring. Being the mountain man that my husband is, he wasn't worried in the least. He began to talk of ways to purify the water in the mud puddles we were passing if it came to that. I was not amused. All I could think about was the cool, refreshing water back at the cabin that I was dying to drink. We made it back to the cabin, and water was the only thing on my mind. I think I guzzled over a liter of water in a matter of minutes. I was desperate to quench my thirst. This triggered my memory back to this verse. How much do I thirst for the things of God? Do I even thirst to such a degree that I'm desperate for Him like I was desperate for that water? Is my life characterized by a hunger and thirst for righteousness?

We were created with basic needs—food, water, and shelter are a few. We were also created to be in relationship with our Creator. When that relationship is not tended, when it's starved, joy, satisfaction, and ultimately blessing seem to vanish. There's an emptiness, a void. We were never meant to live outside of that relationship with God. When we try to, we lack the blessing this verse describes. Under normal circumstances, we wouldn't think about going without food and water for a day or even days on end. So, why do we not think twice about going without our spiritual food? Daily time with God is vital to our faith. It's our sustenance. When we attempt to go without it, we proceed to live powerless lives, constantly craving but never truly satisfied. More than once God has taught me this hard lesson. I must be in regular communication and fellowship with the Lord. I need His Word. I need to read it, to meditate on it, to memorize it. I need time in prayer. This is how God speaks to me. I find it best when I start my day with God. Prioritizing Him in my day results in my day being blessed and my mind being filled with truth. Prayer throughout the day is crucial. Prayer was never intended to be limited to thirty seconds before meals and a quick closing to your day before you fall asleep. Prayer is a lifestyle; it's a conversation with God that is meant to be continuous. Pray without ceasing. As these things become more of a consistent reality in my life, I experience satisfying joy and abundant blessing.

It's always incredible when I come across a promise in God's Word. In this case, it's a promise of His blessing and our satisfaction if we choose to hunger and thirst for righteousness. Being reminded of what is available to me as I walk in obedience with God is what I need to propel me forward in my faith.

I. Describe a time when you hungered and thirsted for more of God in your life.

2. How have you personally experienced Matthew 5:6 to be true?

3. *Journal a prayer of response to the Lord. If you're lacking this hunger and thirst for more of Him, confess that now. If you're experiencing His blessing because of your constant need for Him, thank Him now.*

Day Five
HER STORY

"Stories of how God has changed lives aren't intended to glorify sin; they are meant to glorify God's grace."

—Liz Curtis Higgs, *Bad Girls of the Bible*

Her Story today comes in two parts. God has been at work in her life in phenomenal ways over the past several years, and so we'll just start at the beginning. It's a story of one redeemed soul living daily under God's grace and experiencing the fullness of His blessings. This is her story...

Born into a loving, Christian home, she was raised to believe the truth of the Bible. At the young age of six, she dedicated her life to Jesus Christ through obedience in baptism. Despite her faith in God, she didn't fully grasp what it meant or rather what it looked like to be a Christian. As she puts it, "I loved God, but I didn't really know how to live for Him." So, she perfected the double life. She was a good Christian girl at church and for the most part at home to please her parents, but when she was away from those influences, she began to flirt with the deceiving pleasures of sin. It all started very innocently in her mind. She just hung out with the bad kids, but she wasn't actually doing the things they were doing. This is how she justified her behavior. She could be with them, even be a part of their group, but still be good, right? As the years went on, she found it increasingly difficult to be in the world but not of it. It just got too hard to avoid the temptations. Everyone was drinking, all of her friends were having sex, and most were doing drugs. She began to question why she kept holding out. What was she waiting for? Who was she trying to please? What did she really believe anymore? She was tired of straddling the fence. She was done trying to be both girls. So, she stopped trying. She gave in. She walked away from God.

It was around this time that her dad got a new job, and as a result her family packed up and moved hours away...right before her senior year of high school. She was established in her old school. She knew everyone. Now, she had to start over. It just seemed much easier to make friends by trying to fit in and be just like everyone else. If the kids at her new school were doing drugs, so would she. That was the best way she knew how to make friends anyway. The pressures increased as she went through her final year of high school. By this point, God was barely a fleeting thought in her mind. Her parents felt so bad for uprooting her that they no longer pressured her to attend church with them, and that was the only out she needed. She no longer felt any need for God in her life. If you asked her then, she'd probably tell you she was still a Christian, but God didn't play a role in her life at all. She had removed all godly influence from her life and was perfectly content with that. Prayer and Bible reading were things of her past, and her present was all about the next high. Drugs became a bigger part of her life. As high school was nearing an end, she didn't want to be the only one that hadn't already indulged in sex, so she gave her purity away too. She figured that since she was about to go off to college and she would be having sex then, why not now? She lived for the moment, and she pushed down the guilt she felt, knowing that this was not the life God had intended for her.

College picked up right where high school left off. She found people like her and did what they did. Drugs, alcohol, and sex mixed with a college track career all became a part of her reality. When she was nineteen, she met a boy. She fell for him fast. She thought she loved him, so she gave herself to him in every way. It was summer love. It felt like romance, and it felt good...for the moment, but it came to a screeching halt the moment she found out that she was pregnant. Young, unmarried, school still ahead of her, and a promising future in track. It all seemed to come crashing down on her in a moment. She was so far from God by this time, that keeping the baby wasn't even an option to her. She had to get rid of it. Now, you need to understand that she was that girl just a few years before who took a public stand against abortion and valued waiting until marriage to have sex. But so much had changed. She didn't even know that girl anymore. No one did. She had blocked out everything that she had ever learned about God. She had to in order to live this life. She had fully submitted herself to the world and found it almost easy to make the decision to abort her child. No one tried to talk her out of it. Once it was over, she had a sense of relief in a way. She had gotten away with it. The problem was gone. In her refusal to deal with what she had done, she immersed herself further into a life of drugs. Times between highs were short lived. Life became darker, but she did everything she could to pretend that she was fine, that everything was OK. She threw herself into track workouts. As the weeks went on, however, things still didn't seem right. She was gaining weight, and she became the slowest runner on her team. All the while, she continued in her drug addiction trying to numb the pain inside. About twelve weeks after her abortion, she found out she was still pregnant. Everything suddenly became very clear. She knew she had done wrong. God had wanted her to keep that baby. And as if she had never walked away from God, she felt His presence in her life again for the first time in years. But she was terrified. Panic set in. How could this be? Did they make a mistake? I thought I took care of this? Fear plagued her as she called the abortion clinic with her concerns. They told her to come in immediately. Through examination, the doctor explained to her that she had conceived twins, but they had only successfully removed one. They tried to usher her fears away with "Don't worry, we'll take care of this." She wanted to keep the baby but rationalized those thoughts away as she thought about her wild living the past several weeks. Would the baby even be normal, healthy? Due to how far along she was in her pregnancy, there was only one doctor that was willing to perform the abortion, but they promised to take care of everything and even cover the cost. She would need to return right after Christmas.

Somehow, she managed to make it through Christmas with her family, hiding everything that was going on inside of her. She was overcome with grief at the decision she was about to make, again. As her family went to bed, she proceeded to smoke as much weed as she could to calm her racing thoughts and her aching heart, but the pain would not go away. She had never felt more alone, and as she lay on the bathroom floor with tears streaming down her face, she cried out to God for the first time since she was a child. Through her weeping, she told God how sorry she was for what she was about to do, and she pleaded with Him to wrap His arms around her. She needed Him more than she ever had. She was desperate in her pain. And God met her in her darkest hour. Despite her life of sin that led to this point, in that moment she felt God wrap her in His loving arms and quiet her heart. God knew what she was about to do the very next day, but He loved her still and held her through the night.

The recovery from the second abortion was long and hard. The ache inside was still so strong that drugs seemed to be the only sedative. It was one night in the middle of another high that she found herself telling a hurting friend about God's love. The memory of God holding her on the bathroom floor flooded into her mind, and she realized that His love had changed her. His love had saved her. She left her life of drugs, and picked up a Bible for the first time in years. She began to read verses she had underlined when she was just a child. At the same time, she was employed for an elderly couple that loved her and constantly poured the love of Jesus into her life. God was tugging at her heart. The more she read His Word, the more convicted she was about living out her faith. She could no longer just say she believed in God. Her life needed to reflect that belief. She needed to remove the weeds from her life in order to grow. She knew what her weeds were. She had no godly influences in her life, only friends who brought her down. As she pursued God, her old life satisfied her less and less. Letting her old habits and lifestyle die was a hard process, but she was falling deeper in love with Jesus. That was all she needed.

Even though she was living a new life committed to Christ, shame and guilt from her past decisions haunted her. Through new friendships at her church, she was invited to join a recovery Bible study for women to walk her through the healing process from her abortions. For the longest time, she felt bound by the fact that she would never be able to forgive herself. Her healing came through this truth: she didn't have to, God already had. It wasn't about her or what she had done; it was about what God had done for her on the cross. He bled and died for her and covered her shame with His blood. She was forgiven, and that truth set her free. She was finally able to embrace God's forgiveness, and for the first time she was free to live in His grace. The healing process was the most painful thing she ever went through because she had to uncover the wounds she had worked so hard to bury. Coming to know God's love for her though was worth every painful step.

As difficult as it is for her to re-live her past, she has committed to the Lord to share her story every opportunity she can if it will help someone else find the healing she now knows. It is a daily choice for her to reject the lies of Satan, to refuse his influence over her thoughts and emotions, and to embrace God's truth, but she will never turn back. She is now a new creation; the old has gone. She never thought God could use her after all that she had done to sabotage her life, but each new day she is overwhelmed by His mercy and His grace. She is actively involved in student ministry and is using her story to impact the lives of teenagers through a program called Vantage. She loves God with all her heart. She has been redeemed and called by name. She is a recipient of God's grace. Her story is beautiful because Jesus signed His name over it in blood.

HER STORY—PART 2

"The LORD will guide you always; He will satisfy your needs in a sun-scorched land and will strengthen your frame. You will be like a well-watered garden, like a spring whose waters never fail."

—Isaiah 58:11

So, we meet again on the pages of Her Story today. Fast forward several years, and we begin with part two of Her Story, a beautiful story of God's redeeming love in rescuing one of His daughters. The beauty of her story is that it hasn't ended yet. God is still at work in her life, molding and shaping her into the woman He desires for her to be.

One of the major, life-changing events in part one of her story that was left out was a broken engagement just a few years ago. She had been walking with the Lord for a few years when she was reunited with a young man that she knew in high school. He was also on the path of finding Jesus Christ and turning his life around. Their dating relationship led to engagement, and she found herself immersed in wedding plans and bridal showers. Hidden beneath the surface, though, were some deep issues that began to tear the two of them apart. Just six weeks before their wedding date, they broke off their engagement and cancelled the wedding. Invitations had already been sent out. Gifts had already been given. Reservations had already been made. Yet, God continued to make it very clear to her that this was not the man He had for her. Although she knew she made the right decision, it was no less difficult. The pain, the loss, the feelings of rejection...would she ever be good enough to be loved for who she was? Would anyone ever be able to see past all her stuff and choose to embrace her and love her?

The next year of her life would prove to be a long, hard road of choosing obedience over comfort. God had done so much in her life up until this point that there was no way she was going to walk away from Him now. But it wasn't easy. She graduated from college, and moved away from friends, family, and home once again, choosing to follow God to where He was leading her. This is the part of her story that I love remembering, and I love telling. There is something so incredibly beautiful about watching God's hand of blessing and favor be placed on someone's life, someone who is daily choosing to walk in obedience to His Word. That first year after her broken engagement was a year of fully relying on the Lord. She became devoted to reading and studying God's Word. She dove into Bible study and prayer. The more she exposed herself to the truth of God's Word, the more healing God brought into her life. She was still single and still desperately wanting to be married to the right man, but she was finally returning to her first love, Jesus Christ. I remember seeing such a change in her within that first year... her tone in conversation, her attitude, even her appearance had a new glow. She was radiating Jesus. She was reflecting Him into every part of her life. God was restoring her.

It was just after that first year that God brought an amazing man into her life. It could have almost seemed that Stu came out of nowhere, but it was a divine appointment in God's perfect timing. While God was at work in Rachel's life the previous year bringing healing to her brokenness, He was also at work in Stu's life, preparing Him to be the godly husband that Rachel would need. You might say that there aren't two people on this earth more perfectly suited for each other. Their similarities and differences mix together to make the perfect match. I remember the first time I met Stu, months before he "popped the question", and I knew in my heart that this was the one that Rachel had been waiting for. Like no man before in her life, Stu has loved Rachel with a love like Christ loves His church. Fully aware of her past, he has chosen to lavish her with his love and embrace her as his greatest gift. Looking at their story, I can't help but see how it reflects God's love for us. We continue to wander and stray from His perfect love, but He calls us back to Himself time and time again by His mercy and in His grace. Stu isn't perfect, but he's perfect for Rachel. This past summer, we had the joy of witnessing them be united as one in marriage. Beauty from ashes. Blessing from brokenness. This is our God.

Rachel, there are few others in my life that display the love of Jesus like you do. Your ability to extend grace, love, and forgiveness astounds me. Your willingness to be teachable and moldable, always the student of God's Word, blesses me more than you know. I know you think that I have taught you so much about the love of our God, but He has used you in my life to bring me to my knees time and time again. Thank you for your friendship that I'm confident will last a lifetime. I am so grateful for you. I love you, dear friend.

Your Story

In what specific ways have you experienced God's blessings in your life as you've walked in obedience with Him? What is your blessing story?

About the Author

Loving Jesus and making Him known is Cherie's passion. Playing even a minor role in bringing others closer to Him is her greatest joy. She wants to be found on her knees at His feet in constant and passionate pursuit of Him.

Cherie is married to the man of her dreams, and as she always says, "Jeremy is one of my favorite blessings." Their only child is a giant, fluffy cat named Roxanne. Born and raised in Chicago, she is a lover of big cities. Coffee is her drug of choice. In her opinion, there's nothing quite like time spent with treasured girlfriends. She loves snowboarding and goes as often as she can. She is crazy about the mountains of Arizona, the blizzards of a Midwest winter, reading a great book cuddled up by a fire, and her 15 best friends. She loves writing about what God has done and teaching His Word to anyone who will listen.

In 2011, Cherie founded a women's ministry called Neue Thing, and it exists to teach modern women God's Word by equipping them to believe it, inspiring them to live it, and empowering them to take it and transform a new generation through a vintage faith for Jesus Christ. For something neue, visit **NEUETHING.ORG**.